PST & Indian Gymnasts

Dr. Malika Sharma

Dr. Lalit Sharma

Published by

PST & Indian Gymnasts

ISBN 978-93-86176-89-9

Authors

Dr. Malika Sharma

Dr. Lalit Sharma

Bonfring

309, 2nd Floor, 5th Street Extension, Gandhipuram,

Coimbatore-641 012.

Tamilnadu, India.

E-mail: info@bonfring.org

Website: www.bonfring.org

Phone: 0422 4213231

I Dedicate This Piece Of Work To

God, my Family

And my respected mentor.

I am honored to have you in my life. Thank you for giving me chance to improve myself through all my walks of life…

Acknowledgement

During the journey of writing this Book, I received support and help from many people and here I would like to make an effort to web some words, expressing my gratitude and heartfelt thanks to all of them.

In particular, I am profoundly indebted to my Mentor, **Dr. Lalit Sharma**, Associate Professor, I would like to express my gratitude to him for being a tremendous mentor for me. He has been encouraging my research work and allowing me to grow professionally by his helpful suggestions and time to time technical discussions. Without his priceless advice, guidance, persistent help and invaluably constructive criticism, this Book would not have been possible. I sincerely thank him for making it all worth by showing his passion specifically, for PST for the Gymnasts. I find myself fortunate to have him as my Mentor, as he challenged me with his elevated expectations for the quality of research work and carved me out of my stumbled work to blaze in future life.

I would also like to express my heartfelt gratitude to, **Dr. Sandeep Tiwari**, Associate Professor and **Dr. Sandhya Tiwari**, Associate Professor for offering me expert direction, constant technical guidance and encouragement to ensure progress in my research work and me as in person. I will not leave the opportunity to thank **Dr. Meenakshi**, whose firm support in the study is deeply appreciated for helping me in analyzing the data and drawing the results using statistical techniques, I am grateful for her corporation and providing me with her valuable time.

I would like to express my appreciative thanks to **Mr. PawanBhoir**, who showed kindness and generosity by allowing me to execute my experimental research work at Bhoir's Gymkhana and collect research data from center's Gymnasts, I truly appreciate his positive outlook towards research and letting me make my experiment research work a success.

Special thanks has to be directed to all the **Gymnasts**, those who voluntarily devoted their time and patience for PST program and showed their personal interest and zeal to learn the Psychological Skills for gaining the benefits out of the training imparted.

I cannot go without mentioning and acknowledging by expressing my warm thanks to **Mr. Praveen Sharma** and **Mr. Rahul Sharma**, I feel privileged to have both the pillars and their support by providing me with Gymnastics specific critical knowledge by discussing the relevant issues, intellectual help by constructive criticism, which kept me gleaned and also for moral support.

And finally, but not least, a treasure of love and thanks goes to my whole **family and Friends,** who have been an important and indispensable source of spiritual support, love and motivation throughout my Research work. Above all, I wholeheartedly thank my **mighty God** for giving me the vision, power, spirit and endurance to complete this interesting research.

Chapter	Contents	Page No

Chapter	Contents	Page No
1	**Introduction**	1
	1.1. Psychological Skills Training (PST)	1
	1.2. Sports Psychology a Science-Physiological basis of Body-Mind Relationship	3
	1.3. Cognitive Functions in Sports	3
	1.4. Gymnastics Another Edge of Sports	6
	1.5. Psychological Skills	10
2	**Review of Related Literature**	20
3	**Procedure & Methodology**	23
	3.1. Selection of Subjects	23
	3.2. Selection of Variables	24
	3.3. Criterion Measures	25
	3.4. Development of Training Program	25
	3.5. Administration of Training Program	26
	3.6. Development of Logbook	28
	3.7. Collection of Data	28
	3.8. Procedure for the Assessment of Gymnastics Performance and Psychological Skills	29
	3.9. Statistical Techniques	31
4	**Data Analysis**	33
	4.1. Findings	33
5	**Summary, Conclusion and Recommendations**	102
	5.1. Summary	102
	5.2. Conclusion	109
	5.3. Recommendations	111
	References	112

CHAPTER-1

INTRODUCTION

The domain of sports competition is developing every day so the athletes nearly have the same physical abilities and have different mental skills. Therefore, it is eminent to consider the role of Sports Psychology and mental skills to achieve maximum performance. Sport psychology is the study of the effect of psychological and emotional factors on sport performance, and the effect of sport involvement on psychological and emotional factors. The psychological and emotional factors can be fine-tuned and learned to have a positive effect on sports performance along with overall psychological and emotional makeup, Cox, H. Richard. (2002). Furthermore, some researchers revealed that mental training is the most effective way to improve sport performance, Greenspan, M.J. and D.L. Feltz, 1989; Vealey, R.S., 1994; Weinberg, R.S. and W. Comar, 1994.

We have skimped over the mental aspect of sports performance. Across the world we see athletes, spend thousands of hours perfecting their physical performance but they often neglect their training in mental skills, which should essentially be a part of sport training. Understand the fact that, Physical skills, physical fitness and mental skills are the building blocks of the complete athlete to produce outstanding sports performances. Virtually, our body makes the brain possible but it's our brain that makes the body function.

Evidently, at the top level of sport, many athletes' shows equal physical abilities, the difference between a great performance and a good performance or between winning and losing is often related to mental rather than physical abilities among them. Studies have made it apparent that mental skills play an important role in achieving excellence in sport, Harris, D.V. and B.L. Harris, (1984); Morris, T. and S. Koehn, (2004).

1.1. Psychological Skills Training (PST)

The concept "Psychological Skills" may be briefly unpacked as; "Psychology", as the study and the use of human bio-psycho-social-cultural-spiritual experiences and behavior. "Skill" refers to learnable and trainable abilities used by different individuals in different situations and in diverse ways on the daily basis, (Weinberg and Gould, 2007). Psychological Skill Training (PST) can be explained as a systematic and consistent practice of mental or psychological skills, using a number of different techniques with an objective of enhancing performance, increasing enjoyment, or achieving greater Sport and Physical activity

Self-Satisfaction by Improved Attention, Concentration, Arousal Regulation, Relaxation, Confidence Enhancement, Goal Setting, Self-Talk, and Imagery etc., designed individually, combination of methods selected to attain psychological skill needs (Gill, 2000).

Numerous positive results have been observed from the studies, using different packages (comprising different variables and techniques e.g Attention, Concentration, Arousal Regulation, Relaxation, Confidence Enhancement, Goal Setting, Self-Talk, and Imagery) of PST, on the different subjects, for altogether different durations.

However, despite each PST program being unique, a general structure of three phases has to be followed, namely, Education Phase, The Acquisition Phase and The Practice Phase Hodge, (2007), Weinberg and Gould, (2011).

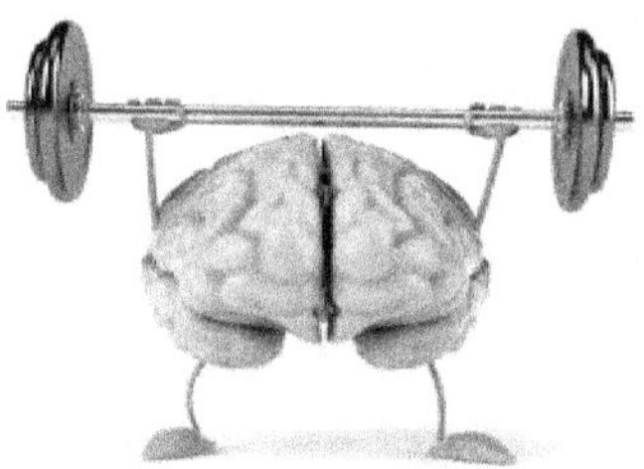

Brain is Trainable

Source-medicalexpress.com

The Education Phase: makes the athletes to understand about the importance and benefits of PST training to their performance.

The Acquisition Phase: focuses on learning the methods for acquiring and developing the different psychological skills.

The Practice Phase: is the longest phase, "when the athlete just practices the methods that are relevant to them.

PST is imperative because psychological factors are the primary key in day-to-day fluctuations in sport performance (i.e., having a good day or an off day). However, they are often over looked because of lack of knowledge about them, misunderstandings about how they are learned, and conception of lack of time. Some queries get upraised, if, PST really train our mind? Does it actually help in modifying behavioral patterns among athlete?, What help them perform at their level best and how? etc. To comprehend the functioning of PST, scientific aspect of the sports psychology needs to be understood.

1.2. Sports Psychology a Science-Physiological Basis of Body-Mind Relationship

An athlete is an excellent portrayal of the complex interaction between mind and the body that interest particularly those of us in psychology. With its success measured in a behavioral outcome, it provides an arena for the study of human performance and psychological characteristics as well as group dynamics, organizational behavior and individual personality characteristics etc. In this segment, some research studies are cited to clear the clouds of doubts and bring the clear understanding of relationship existing between mind and body. Training assists in physiological changes and directly influences the sports performance, since practice brings perfection.

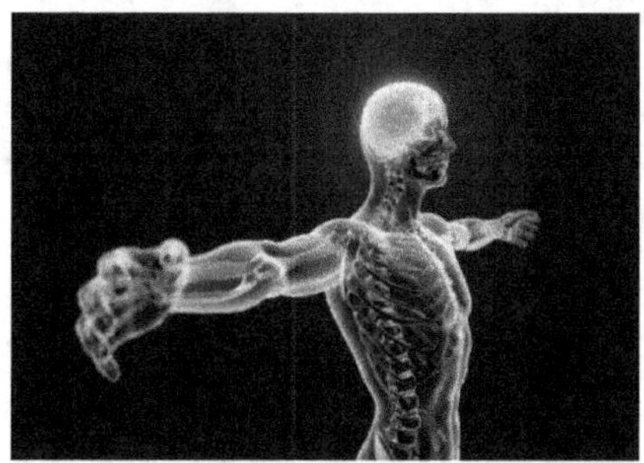

Body Makes the Brain Possible, but Brain Makes the Body Function

Source-psychologytoday.com

Psychological interventions are no magic to improve the sports performance, it slowly changes the thought process or we can say it helps in bringing the automatization in brain functioning, by helping in changing the thought patterns we follow. Cognitive-behavior is most commonly used approach and received the most attention in research. These approaches are drawn from an area of psychotherapy known as cognitive behavior therapy. The key assumption behind this approach is that our *thoughts determine our feelings and behavior.* If we can enhance or positively alter our cognitive processes, our behavior will improve. Thus, understanding of cognitive aspect of sport becomes essential.

1.3. Cognitive Functions in Sports

Cognitive generally refers to processing in the covert physio-psychological systems of man. Cognition processes involves the transformation of sensory input, reduced, elaborated, stored, recovered, and used (Neisser 1967). It includes such complex mental activities as using language, thinking, remembering, conceptualizing, imagining, learning, information processing, and mental manipulation of symbols (Houston, Bee, Hatfield, and Rim 1979).

Success of an athlete in the arena of competitive sports depends largely on his/her cognitive functions. For overpowering, the rival in the hours of contest, a sportsperson, requires correct goal setting and decision-making. Cognitive functions like accurate perception, memorization of rules and regulations, retentions of motor learning gains, and insightful behavior in developing strategies and applying tactics, help fulfilling the said requirements. Effective synchronization of motor skill and cognitive skills takes place during practice sessions in presence of coach. In practice, sessions the learners get ample opportunities to perform skillfully and guide own performance through self-evaluation. Cognitive-Behavioral Therapy (CBT), is a system of psychotherapy that attempts to reduce excessive emotional reactions and self-defeating behavior by modifying the imperfect thinking and maladaptive beliefs that underlie these reactions. CBT has elicited much interest in the treatment of psychological problems both in and outside the realm of sport. It aim to alter dyes functional thoughts either directly via cognitive techniques or indirectly through behavioral techniques.

CBT is based on the idea that problems aren't caused by situations themselves, but by how we interpret them in our thoughts. These thoughts in return affect our feelings and actions. It is also understood as a talking therapy which assists to deal problems by altering the way of thinking and its outcome behavior. It doesn't remove the problems, but aids to manage them in a more positive way. It supports to test and understand the actions that can affect how one think and feel. It appears to be a practical approach to improve one's state of mind on a day to day basis.

There is an interconnection between thoughts, feelings, physical sensations and actions. CBT assists stop these negative cycles with the purposes to break down factors that make us feel bad, anxious or scared so that they are more manageable. It shows how to change negative patterns to improve the way we feel. A change in thinking (cognitive) and doing (behavior) is possible by talking. The change in behavior can make one feel better about life. The dominating areas in CBT are "Goal setting, imagery or mental rehearsal, relaxation training, stress management, self-monitoring, self-instruction, cognitive restructuring, and modeling interventions". These interventions specifically support the behavior change efficacy.

The process of "strengthening positive behaviour and weakening negative behaviour towards a goal" (Behncke, 2004) has meant that CBT is inherently appealing to sport psychologists focusing on performance enhancement in athletes.

As numerous literature support the functioning relationships between cognition and sports performance, benefits of improving confidence and sports performance, within the last few years both sports participants and sports psychologists have become increasingly concerned with cognitive skills. The motor learning is aligned most closely with the psychology areas of cognition, perception and the experimental psychology of learning and performance. As within sports sciences, motor learning tend to focus on cognitive processes involved in the learning and performance of skilled movements, and the cognitive and neuropsychological processes underlying controlled movements has been concluded by Hayes, (1982), physiological, Hasan, Enoka, and Stuart, (1985), peripheral (Zajac, 1993) and central nervous system (Behmand Sale, 1993; Wolpaw, 1994) operation to movement coordination, mediated by different facets of psychological involvement (Bergenheim, Johansson, Granlund, and Pedersen, 1996).

Release Negative thoughts and Behavior, Strengthen Your Brain

Source-psychologytoday.com

The applied sport psychology research aims to improve sport performance by developing effective interventions. In sport psychology, research and practice have been grounded in the action-oriented approach of CBT, as sport psychology consultants often adhere to a psycho-educational approach of teaching psychological skills to athletes. CBT exponents propose that human behavior is a mutual procedure of cognitions, feelings, and behaviors (Corey, 2009), with cognition proposed as the most prominent facet of human behavior (Walen, DiGiuseppe, and Dryden, 1992). Cognitive behavioral theorists contend that the most effective way to overcome distress and improve athletic performance is to change thought patterns as distress is the result of dysfunctional thinking. Keeping in view the theoretical underpinnings of CBT, it is suggested by several researchers to apply and use PST in the sport domain, (Brown, 2011).

Application and tailoring of PST and other specific training programs, to a great extent depends on the nature of sports and therefore it is essential to know the very nature of the sport on which PST will be applied.

1.4.   Gymnastics Another Edge of Sports

Gymnastics is much more than what we see at the Olympics. It is governed by the Federation of International Gymnastics and consists of several disciplines, Artistic, Rhythmic, Aerobic, Acrobatic and Trampoline Gymnastics. This study is about Artistic Gymnastics (by using the term gymnastics, Artistic Gymnastics is mentioned). Over the last decade, Artistic gymnastics has developed tremendously. Enormous changes have been seen, for instance complexity of movements on apparatuses has increased. For example, a new vault table with more elasticity, larger surface and more stability replaced the traditional vaulting horse in 2001 for the purpose of safety. Hence, the Gymnasts are capable to perform higher difficult movement and spectacular routines.

Additionally, in 2006, the code of points was modified in such a way that the score of the routine consists of an execution score and a difficulty score. The execution score is 10 points and judges deduct points from it for every error that gymnast make, i.e. falls, wobbles, extra swings, steps, bent arms/legs, low landings, incorrect body positions etc. The difficulty score has no base score and is based on the difficulty of the routine and this score is open-ended. The modification in the code of points has resulted in more challenging and higher difficulty elements routines. Because of these developments, gymnastics is becoming further more spectacular as gymnasts are trying to reach the highest score with the eventual goal to win the championships. To achieve these goals gymnasts have to attain several characteristics in physical and psychological domain. The psychological domain consists of mind related characteristics, including concentration, motivation, striving for perfection, dealing with anxiety and the use of psychological strategies (Waples, 2005; Lavallee and Robinson, 2007; d'Arripe-Longueville, Hars, Debois, and Calmels, 2009).Some of these characteristics will be specifically more important during training (like motivation, striving for perfection and dealing with anxiety) while others will be more important during competition (concentration, confidence and coping with pressure and nerves). Besides several important physical and psychological characteristics, an exposure to the substantial training volumes is required. In gymnastics, it is just gymnast and the competitive arena as Gymnastics is an individual sport, this very nature of Gymnastics makes PST more relevant to it.

Gymnasts require a lot of practice on the apparatuses to grip over the skills and execute them confidently. The structure of apparatuses itself is threatening, on which gymnasts perform air born movements by taking off from legs or hands (involving twists and rotations), releasing and catching the apparatuses, leaping, jumping, hoping, balancing, dancing etc. with execution, beauty, aesthetics, in rhythm and altering directions in the air with in fraction of seconds.

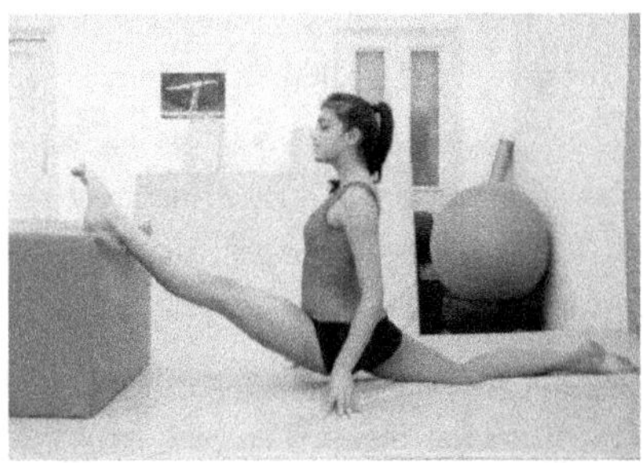

Here are the factors that put gymnasts and gymnastics at the top of the sports hierarchy of difficulty in i.e, Balance, Rotation, Spatial Awareness, Nine times Body Weight Strength, Proprioception and Kinesthetic Awareness, Skill and Routine Timing to Six Thousandths of a Second, Short Distance Sprint Speed of 16+ (20+ for men) Miles per Hour, Tumbling and Vault Heights of 13+ (16+ for men) Feet High and 1080 Degrees and even more of Rotations now being done of Twisting in Less than one second.

Hence, competitive Gymnastics place mental and physical demand on athletes. Execution of difficult skills and highly intensive training denotes the risk of injuries and failure etc. being taken by the gymnast (Caine, Lindner, Mandelbaum, and Sands, 1996; Kerr and Minden, 1988). This gymnast's fear and perception of risk, understandably may result of being injured while competing and/or learning a new skill as some times the injuries in gymnastics can be life threatening. Fear of injury can produce detrimental effect on a gymnast's performance and self-confidence. Researches in Sport psychology have shown that fear of injury is a common source of worry and a possible source for quitting competition among young gymnasts (Duda, 1995; Duda and Gano-Overway, 19986; Klint and Weiss, 1986; Weiss, Weise, and Klint, 1989).

Lack of confidence in their ability to perform successfully leads to fear of injury and fear of failure. Control over fearful situations is necessary in order to perform at high competitive levels. In order to overcome fear, gymnasts need to adopt self-enhancing perspectives rather than self-defeating ones. Therefore, Psychological Skills Training could be designed to fulfill individualized requirements. While using these approaches, athletes learns to focus on relevant information, such as, feeling relaxed to perform their best, rather than worrying about the possibility of being injured. These strategies, not only improves concentration, but may also permit athlete to gain control over their fears and increase self-confidence for performing difficult skills. These skills are trainable and can be inculcated in young children and adolescents (Weiss, 1991). Therefore, these techniques have been incorporated in PST schedule designed by scholar. The objective of this study is to test the effect of psychological skills program on gymnasts, by providing an effective PST to competitive gymnasts, to overcome their fears and mental blocks.

The roots of gymnastics and, indeed, the roots of almost every other sport, originate in the body's Fundamental Movement Patterns. Every single skill in gymnastics discipline evolves from one or more of these movement patterns: Landings, Static Positions, Locomotion's, Rotations, Swings, Springs and Object Manipulation. In additions to the above mentioned dynamics, there are numerous other areas where gymnasts must exceed all other athletes: Strength to Body Weight Ratio, Leg, Back and Shoulder Flexibility, Female Upper Body Strength, Explosive Power, Kinesthetic air sense and awareness, Focus, Concentration and Pressure Competitions, (Gymnastics Zone, 2011), (http:gymnasticszone.com). Various apparatuses have their own scientific and anatomical structures. Depending on the peculiarity of the apparatuses, different level and type of physical and mental demands needs to be met by a gymnast for successful performances.

Each apparatus in gymnastics requires different physical attributes and mental capabilities to excel. Since, each player has to perform number of apparatus, therefore, should be physical and mentally sound enough to meet the challenges of each apparatus.

Vault (Men and women): Vaulting to Success by Using Mental Strategies: It is a single element that is over in a matter of seconds. Because entire score depends on this one element, vault some-times have an all-or-nothing feel to it, so, they need to be completely focused as they vault. On the other hand, many competitors enjoy vault because they just do it without much time to let their thinking get in the way of performance. Some of the useful skills are Imagery to set the path of the movements, managing anxiety to perform in optimal state and Energizing to perform vault with power and amplitude.

Floor Exercise (Men and Women) tumbling to the top: Often gymnasts experience anxiety about competing on floor as gymnasts have to perform a number of acrobatic and dance elements in the period of 70-90 seconds. Missing/falling in even a single move may devastate the performance. It requires mental focus and activation control for gymnasts to perform their best. Women must mentally switch from powerful tumbling to the relatively more restful and graceful dance portions, all with flow and continuity. Mental Strategies that gymnasts must use are energized breathing, energized imagery, or upbeat music.

Imagery for remembering the routine. Floor requires lot of concentration power, the ability to shift focus quickly. Gymnasts needs to go from narrow/internal (being aware of the body position) to narrow/external (looking at the corner of the mat where they will do their next tumbling pass) to broad/external (expressions to the judges) and rapidly need to switch back and forth throughout the routine.

Uneven parallel Bars: needs a moderate amount of physical and mental energy to maintain her swing. She must learn to focus and concentrate to do a variety of moves in the right position to grasp the bar. Some of the important mental skills are Imagery, arousal regulation and Managing fear on Bars.

Balance Beam: it is often seen as the most difficult event. Just staying on the beam sometimes becomes a primary goal. It is easy to slip and fall and even easier to have a major wobble. Inability to control anxiety can be a gymnast's downfall on beam more than on the other events. In addition, fear is a major factor and can increase the anxiety. It is not surprising with all the aerial moves that fear of injury can hamper a gymnast's beam progress and performance. Mental skills to be used are Anxiety Management, Focus Strategies, and Imagery etc.

Pommel Horse: Like women's balance beam, pommel horse is often considered the most difficult event for men, especially in competition. For this event, the gymnast must stay calm and not get too psyched up. He must be able to focus and block out distractions. Too much activation will make routine fell out of control, and then gymnasts are more likely to fall, especially in competition. A few deep breaths before a routine can help gymnast to relax in competition. Here anxiety management and specific relaxation skills must be used along with Focusing and Imagery.

Roman Rings: Because rings Involves so much strength, adrenaline in competition can be a gymnast's best friend. The main mental skill involves harnessing the adrenaline so that it works to your advantage. It requires more calm and balanced mental state with complete concentration. Gymnasts must monitor energy level and use Energizing strategies.

Parallel Bars: It is much like pommel horse in that a gymnast need to their energy, especially in competition. In addition, the more dynamic moves require intense concentration because there is more room for error. Skills to be used are Activation control and Focus.

High Bar: Often the biggest obstacle to overcome on high bar is fear. Good breathing, self-talk, and imagery are very helpful in overcoming anxieties on high bar. In addition, focus is important on high bar, as gymnasts can't just go through the motions as might on some other events because lapses in concentration can lead to more serious falls. Psychological skills to be followed are Anxiety management, Positive self-talk and Focus.

1.5. Psychological Skills

A major tenet of sport and performance psychology is that mental skills are important determinants of performance involving cognitive abilities perfected through mental skills training.

The intent of which is to provide a set of psychological strategies for dedicated improvement of performance, successfully recovering from sport injury, performing learned skills successfully and maintaining a positive life-balance between sport and other aspects of life, including family.

Mental skills are trainable internal capabilities that help an athlete improve performance by learning to control their minds efficiently and consistently as they execute attainable goals. (Gerald S. Graham, 2013).

Sport psychologists have proposed three classifications for mental skills; Foundation Skills consists of goal setting, self-confidence and commitment (Orlick, T., 1992, Bota, J.D., 1993).

Psycho-Somatic Skills consists of stress reaction, fear control, relaxation and activation which have a relationship with physiological traits (Landers, D., S. Boutcher and M. Wang, 1986). Cognitive Skills consist of imagery, mental training, focusing, refocusing and competition planning. These skills are related with cognitive processes such as learning, perception, memory and thinking (Mayer, R.E., 1992, Stevenson, M., 1999).

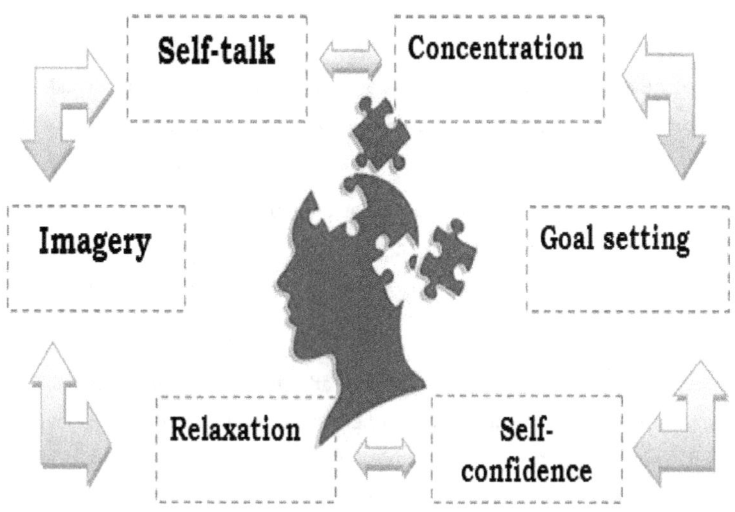

Interrelated Psychological Skills

All Psychological skills are interrelated with each other and organize a unique, composite, inseparable whole (Weinberg and Gould, 2007). It can incorporate a number of different mental skills. A large number of empirical studies have focused on individual psychological skills and their effect on performance, including confidence, motivation, attention, visualization, and psychosomatic skills (Gucciardi, Gordon, and Dimmock, 2009). Likewise, some data presents the use of mental skills (goal setting, imagery, relaxation, and self-talk)is an important area in the field of sport psychology (Vealey, 2007; Williams and Harris, 2001). Within a specified time limit goal setting can increase performance during competition. Moreover, imagery as using all the senses to re-make or make an involvement in the psyche helps athletes to perform better and increase self-confidence (Rattanakoses, et al., 2009).

Furthermore, relaxation technique assist to rid the muscles tension, interfering with performance and help to relax body and mind. It also promotes confidence by decreasing the effect of undesirable thoughts and feelings. In addition, self-talk is occurring statements about something as well as increase performance and skills in sport (Howland, 2006; Vealey, 2007). Optimal attention is considered to be a very important component for success in sport (Maynard and Howe, 1989) and Weinberg and Gould (2007) stated that self-confidence can be beneficial to athletes, since it facilitates positive emotions and concentration, setting challenging goals and increasing effort, and that it has a positive effect on game strategies, psychological momentum and performance. On the facts claimed and understanding the problems of the gymnasts and on the basis of above discussion on gymnasts and the mental demands made on them, the following psychological skills were selected for the present study, mental Imagery, Relaxation, Attention, Goal setting, self-confidence, and Self-talk.

Each skill should be developed keeping in mind the individual skill level, each psychological skill and individual requirement play an important role to prepare athlete for the better performance. Hence, it is essential to understand every single psychological skill individually.

Relaxation

Sports field is cluttered with broken dreams of athletes whose performance collapsed when they are most needed to be in control of themselves and focus on the task at hand. It is common to see athletes "freeze" in big games, training and commit unexplainable error during performances.

Incapability of athletes to perform well in relation to their abilities, nervousness in anticipation of the sporting challenges could be the root cause of anxiety.

In modern sports psychology, the problem anxiety is an urgent matter of concern. It has been realized that in anxiety, psychological factors play an important role during competitions as in competitive sports, every athlete go through anxious feeling before, during and after competitions, Lizuka, (2005). Even world's most successful athlete could feel nervous due to anxiety, fear of failure, injury and lacking confidence. Anxiety can be named as worry, an unpleasant emotion when faced with challenging situation, Moran (2004).

The effect of anxiety on performance has been discussed by a number of theories and as there appear to be an reciprocal effect between the amounts of anxiety necessary to perform maximally certain particular task, all theories shows an agreement that maximum performance is reduced by too much anxiety, Hanin (1997). (Yerkes, 1908) Inverted 'U' theory predicts that as arousal increase, performance improves but only to a certain point (top of the Inverted 'U'). But if athlete's arousal increase beyond this point then performance starts diminishes.

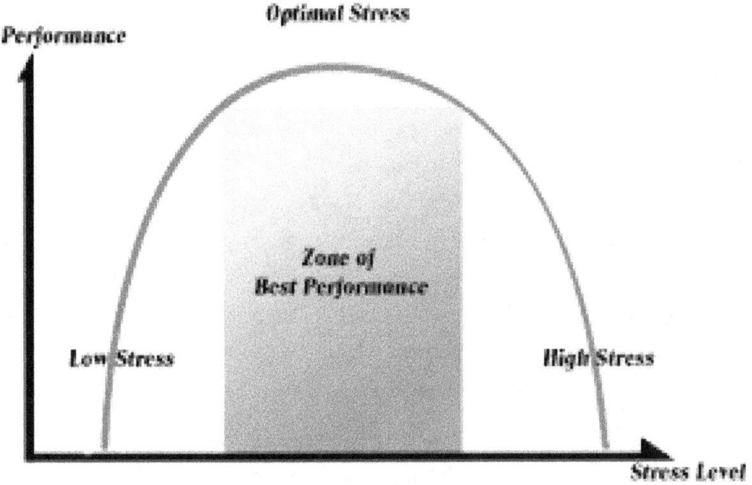

Inverted 'U' Theory

In sport psychology, anxiety refers to an unpleasant emotions characterized by vague but persistent apprehensive feeling and fear before an event. It is a reaction to imminent threat. There are cognitive and somatic sub-components, influencing performance before and during competitions.

Cognitive is the mental component, characterized by negative prospects regarding success or self evaluation, negative self-talk, worry about performance, failure images and distraction (Jervis, 2002). While somatic is a physiological aspect, related to autonomic arousal and harming symptoms (nervousness, high or low blood pressure, dry throat, muscular tension, rapid heart rate and butterflies in the stomach) (Martens et al 1990), Karageorghis (2007).

Relaxation manage athlete's physical energy levels and to enable good performance, (Vealey, 2007) and reduces unwanted muscular tension, reduce extreme activation of the sympathetic nervous system and mind is calm by keeping it productively occupied, Burton and Raedeke (2008). Even researchers agreed that successful elite athletes regularly use relaxation technique to manage their physical energy (Howland, 2006; Neiss, 1988; Williams and Harris, 2001) and Coaches recognized the importance of relaxation in competitive winner, often encouraging athletes either to relax or to "psych up" if they want to be more successful. Some of the techniques, incorporated in to training schedule were Somatic Anxiety reduction

Techniques including Progressive muscles, Breath Control, Abdominal/Diaphragmatic Breathing, Two-to-One breathing, Biofeedback and Cognitive-Anxiety Reduction–to relax the mind involved Meditation, Body scan meditation, Mindfulness, Visualization or guided imagery, Centering and Autogenic Training.

Mental Imagery

Mental imagery is an experience that, significantly resembles the experience of perceiving some object, event, or scene, but that occurs when the relevant object, event, or scene is not actually present to the senses i.e "seeing in the mind's eye," "hearing in the head," "imagining the feel of," etc. Imagery is an experience similar to a sensory experience (visual, kinesthetic, auditory, tactile and olfactory). It involves moods and emotions, but arising in the absence of the usual external stimuli as sensing the movement of your body, apparatus etc. whenever we imagine ourselves performing an action in the absence of physical practice, we are said to be using imagery. It has been increasingly used to enhance motor performance.

Eccles (1958), in a Scientific American article, presented evidence about the workability of the visual imagery as a fact that while imaging precise and perfect performance, it turn in physiologically creating neural patterns in the brain, just as if performed the action physically. These patterns are similar to small tracks engraved in the brain cells which can ultimately enable an athlete to perform physical feats by simply mentally practicing the move. Hence, mental imagery is intended to train our minds and create the neural patterns in our brain to teach our muscles to do exactly what we want them to do.

Sports psychologists have provided numerous theories, **namely** *Psycho neuromuscular Symbolic Learning Theory, The arousal/activation,* combined with actual practice of the skill; imagery is not a replacement for regular gymnastics practice, but instead, it is enrichment. Ungerleider, Steven (1996).

Self-Talk

Self talk is one commonly used strategy and has been defined as "a multidimensional phenomenon concerned with athletes' verbalizations that are addressed to themselves" (Hardy, Hall, and Hardy, 2005).

The use of self-talk plans to control and organize athletes' thoughts has been promoted as a key component for successful sport performance, and self-talk is frequently included as an integral part of psychological skill training (Hardy, Jones, and Gould, 1996). Learning positive self-talk involves Thought Stopping and Thought Replacement.

Concentration

Focus is vital for performing one's best. The real segment of fixation is the capacity to center one's consideration on the current workload and in this manner not be exasperates or influenced by immaterial outer and inward boosts, Wilson, V.E., Peper, E. & Schmid, A. (2006).

Peak performance occurs when athletes are able to voluntarily concentrate on the cues in their environment and perceive them to demand an action that is within their ability to execute.

Most sports require being able to shift between different types of concentration. Athletes need to be able to control the width of their attentional focus (e.g. narrow vs. broad) as well as the direction (e.g. internal vs. external) of their attention. Using width and direction as two dimensions of concentration allows us to separate different attentional skills into one of four categories.

Goal Setting

By knowing precisely what you want to achieve, you know where you have to concentrate your efforts.

The mechanism of the relationship between goals and performance exist on the basis that, High goals lead to greater effort and/or persistence than do moderately difficult, easy, or vague goals. Goals direct attention, effort, and action toward goal-relevant actions at the expense of non relevant actions. Because performance is a function of both ability and motivation, goal effects also depend upon having the requisite task knowledge and skills. Goals may simply motivate one to use one's existing ability, may automatically "pull" stored task-relevant knowledge into awareness, and/or may motivate people to work hard and develop new skills. The latter is most common when people are confronted by new, complex tasks.

Goal setting is used by top-level athletes and achievers in all fields. Setting goals gives long-term vision and short-term motivation. The body, together with the mind, will not reach toward achievement until they have clear objectives. It focuses acquisition of knowledge, attention and helps to organize time and resources. (Wynn Davis, 1998).

Confidence

"Self-confidence," as the term is used here, is the belief that one can successfully execute a specific activity rather than a global trait that accounts for overall performance optimism. Self-confidence is having confidence in oneself. It doesn't essentially infer 'self-conviction' or a faith in one's capacity to succeed.

Rationale of the Study

Effective learning of psychological skills is central to solving and preventing mental health problems, and reaching at the higher level of sports performance. PST if rendered in a systematic manner can yield elevated performances along with achieving greater self-satisfaction. PST is very commonly utilized by overseas sports person in a variety of sports settings as well as at different level of preparations of competition where as in our country the system has not being evolved to incorporate PST at top most level of preparation. Since PST is extremely beneficial in increasing the psychic capacities of the sports person it becomes apparent then to give PST a status of paramount importance. PST is the mental abilities which have to be trained in order to attain success at any level of competition. Looking into the importance and benefits that can be derived as a result of PST it then becomes important to develop and implement the PST Program for different sports and therefore, the research scholar after having gleaned the literature and series of discussion with the advisor and advisory committee members decided to analyze the effect of PST on gymnasts.

Statement of the Problem

Psychological skills training program (PST) is a powerful dimension to the sports performance. The PST program may influence the gymnasts differently to a great extent depending upon the level of performance. Therefore, the purpose of this research, formally may be stated, as to analyze the effect of PST on Performance of the Indian Gymnasts.

Objectives of the Study

Following objectives were set for the study:

1) To assess the effect of PST Program on the psychological skills of the Gymnasts.
2) To know the strength of psychological skills among the Gymnasts.
3) To assess the effect of PST Program on the performance of the Gymnasts.
4) To test the relationship between Psychological Skills and Gymnast's performance
5) To assess the effect of relaxation training on the pulse rate, respiratory rate and tension level of the gymnasts.
6) To test the linear trend in the number of training sessions has affect on the pulse rate, respiration rate and tension level of the gymnasts.
7) To test the linear trend in the number of training sessions has affect on visual, auditory, kinesthetic and mood imagery.
8) To know the effect of PST on self-confidence.
9) To know the effect of psychological Training on attention.

10) Does the self talk training modify thought process from negative thought process to positive thought process?

11) To assess the effect of PST on Goal setting.

Hypothesis

1) Psychological Skills Training Program would have significant effect on the performance of the gymnasts.

2) There would not be a significant effect of intervention program on strengthening the weak psychological skills.

3) There would be a significant affect of each training session on the pulse rate, respiratory rate and tension level.

4) There would be a linear significant trend of Imagery training sessions on visual, auditory, kinesthetic and mood imagery.

Delimitations

1) The study was confined to the sixty male and female Indian players of Artistic Gymnastics.

2) The study was confined to the players who participated at least at district/state level championships.

3) Study was further confined to artistic gymnasts only.

4) Study was further confined to six weeks of training.

Limitation

Individuality of the subjects to understand, cooperate and responses considered as one of the limitations for the study.

Definitions and Explanation of Important Terms

Psychological Skills

These are the mental qualities and abilities. Some athletes have tremendous abilities to psych themselves up for competition, to manage their stress, to concentrate intensely and to set challenging but realistic goals. They have the ability to visualize themselves being successful (Orlick. T,1996).

Relaxation

Mental relaxation is of an entirely different kind inasmuch as it means, in effect, an absence of thinking, of conscious physical relaxation.

Concentration

Concentration is the cognitive process of selectively paying attention to one thing to the exclusion of others.

Confidence

A state of being certain either that a hypothesis or prediction is correct or that a chosen course of action is the best or most effective. Fearlessness is having trust in oneself. Fearlessness does not so much suggest 'self-conviction' or a faith in one's capacity to succeed.

Imagery

Imagery is an experience similar to a sensory experience (seeing, feeling, hearing) but arising in the absence of the usual external stimuli. It is more than just visualizing an experience in mind's eye, involving any or all senses, (Orlick T., 1996).

Goal Setting

It is determining the target to be achieved and a powerful strategy to stay focused for reaching dreams and ambitions (Singh. A, 2007).

Self-Talk

Self-talks are internal dialogues we use to communicate with ourselves, they can influence our inner voices and perceptions. Inner voices can be both good and bad. (Scott, E and M.S, 2008).

Significance of the Study

The results of the study shall be extremely useful in the following ways:

1) Findings of the present study are useful to prepare the PST program, which will enable us to strengthen the psychological skills among the gymnasts.
2) Result will help the coaches to use the PST program to enable their gymnasts to give their best performance.
3) This program may help the gymnasts to learn to handle adversity in practice, confidence can be developed to use similar techniques to manage the stress of situation.
4) Findings may help the coaches to use PST Program for the improvement of other positive psychological characteristics.
5) Findings may help the sport psychologist to understand that how many number of sessions are required to bring out desirous changes.

6) Results will also help to develop individualized PST program for gymnasts.

7) Results will also help us to understand whether single session has positive effect on psychological skills.

8) Psychological skills training will also help the gymnasts to develop skills which will help them to sharpen their life skills also.

CHAPTER-2

REVIEW OF RELATED LITERATURE

Over a century research and practice in Sport psychology have been in existence. It has been in its transition with establishment of first North American sport psychology laboratory in 1925 to its steps in academic discipline. Another wing added with the emergence of the Association for the Advancement of Applied Sport Psychology (AAASP) in 1985, and the Journal of Applied Sport Psychology (1989). Additionally, in 1991, a shift in culture toward competition and winning had been noticed in many territories, which has resulted in increased pressure on athletes and people associated with sports performance, aiming to achieve high performance.

For the enhanced understanding of the psychology and its relation with sports performance, the researchers and scholars have been involved in studying and researching. Greenspan & Feltz (1994) and Vealey (1994) dissected studies that were performed until 1992, presenting that 75 % (9 of 11) studies utilizing mental mediations enhanced execution in a mixed bag of group and individual games. Inside of a same year, Weinberg & Comar (1994) broke down 10 more Study's outcomes demonstrating 8 of 10 had a constructive outcome on execution and self-improvement (Cox, 2007).

Later various factors effecting sports performance were tested, Otten, (2009), Gucciadi, (2010), anxiety, Morris & Kavassanu, (2009), self-confidence, Brown, Malouff, & Schutte, (2005), used various psychological skills training (PST) programs i.e., the systematic and consistent practice of psychological skills enhancing performance, Weinberg & Gould, (2011) to inbuilt athletes with the ability to cope with a innumerable situations in competitions. Though there has been empirical and anecdotal evidence for the effectiveness of PST on sport performance, (Hatzigeorgiadis, Zourbanos, Galanis, & The odorakis, 2011) still a breach in the literature on athlete's or coaches' willingness to use PST programs (Anderson, 2005; Martin, 2005; Massey, Meyer, & Hatch, 2011).Over the past few decades, for actualizing athlete's factual potential, a more precise approach has been applied in competitive sport.

The past researches summarize and highlights the application of various psychological skills training programs at different levels and in different sports, it reveals that psychological aspect plays a role in the development of performance. Self-confidence, self-talk, Imagery, Goal-setting, Relaxation, attention and concentration appears important for successful participation in sports, while there are other numerous psychological skills and strategies are also essential for the excellence in sports. A beneficial development of athletes using PST and sport psychology services has been seen. Thus, the athletes engaged in PST have implications for both talent and performance improvement.

Studies on Psycho logical qualities of apex performers were resumed with a broader overview. It is Apprehended that the good performers exhibits confidence, self-regulate arousal and anxiety, maintain focus, commitment and determination, goal setting, using imagery, coping skills, and develop competition and refocusing plans. Provided that athletes use the psychological skills and strategies to reach at higher performance, the efficacy of interventions to examine the effect of psychological skills on athlete's performance has also been reviewed. Krane and Williams (2009).

Even though we have been witnessing huge research evidences that has sustained a relation between psychological characteristics and performance in sports, (May, Veach, et al, 1985; Morgan & Pollock, 1977; Ogilvie, 1968), but along with that some results have often been controversial since the level of competitive stress, and the ability of an individual to cope with the demands placed by the sports environment, were found to be directly related to the type of sport, the position played in sports, as well as the physical and mental ability of the athlete (Highlen& Bennett, 1983; Nation & LeUnes, 1983; Riddick, 1984), Michael C., (1996). Further research has quantified differences in psychological response between elite versus non elite athletes (Morgan, 1985). However, the difficulty of matching psychological variables with physiological response and the subsequent problems in interpreting these findings are well recognized (Cox, 1985; Smith, Burwitz, & Jakeman, 1988). When conducted a study by Maynard and Howe (1989), he found no differences for attentional control among the elite and non elite players. There has been times when the researchers working in this field could not find any association in them, as, "found no association between psychological skills and increased training volume in elite judo athletes", Murphy, Fleck, et al, (1990), and "no differences in psychological skills between various sports performance levels professional, female tennis players", Meyers, Sterling, et al, (1994).

Now in addition to the coaches, a big group of other individuals like conditioning experts, sports trainers, physiotherapists, physicians, etc function as a support system to actualize the high sports achievements. However, as mentioned above the negligent behavior of the coaches and the athletes towards Sports Psychology is more prevalent in India. No Psychologist assistance has been provided to the player. Players neither feels the requirement of Sports psychologist nor any need of psychological interventions, as they are totally unaware of the mental side of their game and even strengths of their mind which can work miraculously for their sports performance. Here, this acts as a thoughtful interest for the researchers. The main objective of the present study is to examine the Effect of *Psychological Skills Training Program* on The Performance of Indian Gymnasts. Existing literature on PST helps to understand the relationship amongst the various Psychological skills (Relaxation, Goal-setting, Positive Self-talk, Imagery, Attention and Self-confidence) and with the sports performance. These studies also contributed to comprehend the psychological weaknesses and strengths of a sports person, effectiveness of mental training or psychological training for the better sports performance.

The lack of research on the psychological skills of Indian Gymnasts or Indian sports population and its effect on performance makes research on this topic imperative. The subsequent purpose of this study is, therefore, to identify the Effect of Psychological Skills Training Program on the performance of Indian Gymnasts.

CHAPTER-3

PROCEDURE & METHODOLOGY

A well designed research methodology is a back bone for any research. In this chapter selection of subjects, selection of variables, criterion measure, preparation of training program, administration of training, preparation of log book, statistical techniques have been explained.

3.1. Selection of Subjects

For the purpose of the present experimental study the purposive sampling method was used to select the artistic gymnasts as the subjects.

The purposive sampling method is used since only those gymnasts were selected for the purpose of experiment who have had participated at least at district/state championships and higher levels.

By using this method the scholar had selected two groups of 30 gymnasts each from the gymnasts, trainees at the Bhoir Gymkhana, Mumbai, representing the Indian gymnasts population in true manner and served as experimental group and controlled group. The age range of the participants spanned 9 to 17 years and the average mean age of the subjects was 13 years, while years of training ranged between 4-11 years with the average mean training age of 6 years.

All gymnasts participated at least at the district/State/national competitive sub-junior, junior and senior gymnastics championships. While, five elite gymnasts represented India at international level.

Thus, the sixty gymnasts, who later were divided into two equal groups, i.e the experimental Group and control group initially consisted of 30 gymnasts. Voluntarily Gymnasts attended training regularly at Bhoir's Gymnastics center, situated in Mumbai, India.

But in experiment group one gymnast had discontinued due to an injury, she had during the training of gymnastics, while six gymnasts did not turn up for the second trials, from the control group.

Finally, total number of 29 gymnasts completed the training in experimental group and 24 gymnasts completed pre and post trials in control group.

The selection of the subjects has been presented in figure 1.

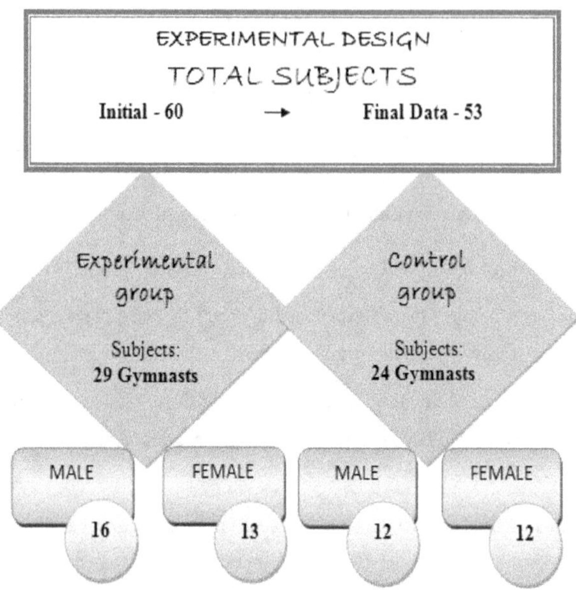

Figure 1: Selection of Subjects

3.2. Selection of Variables

On the premise of accessible writing and different looks into it is said that mental abilities assume a critical part in upgrading the performance of the Gymnast (Bennett and Pravitz, 1982). In the present study Psychological Skill are the independent variables whereas, the performance is the dependent variable. In order, to assess the significant contribution of PST towards the Gymnast's performance, by the means of various mental skills preparation methods providing training in Relaxation, Imagery, Concentration and Goal-setting are used as the important factors. (Bennett and Pravitz, 1982), (Gauron, 1984) and (Unestahl, 1983). In the present study the following psychological skills-Relaxation, Imagery, Attention, self-Confidence, Self-talk and Goal Setting were used for the purpose of the study. Program includes the considerations, such as Educational Session, Skill development, Application and Evaluation. Performance, skill acquisition and Psychological well-being are important variables of the study as on these parameters the scores of the gymnast's before PST and after PST have been evaluated to assess the effect of PST program on the gymnast's performance. Presentation of the variables is presented in figure 2.

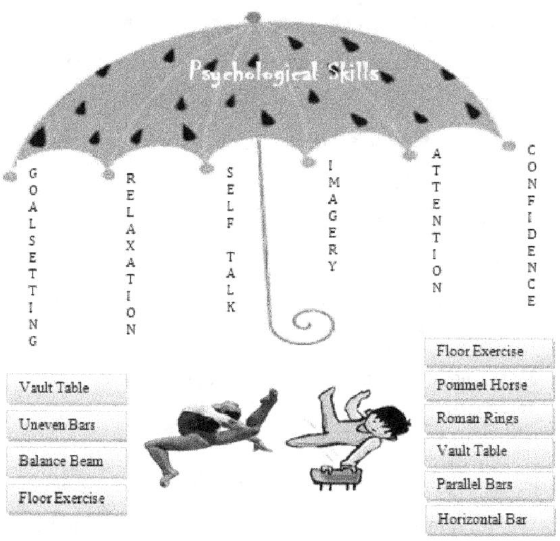

Figure 2: Dependent and Independent Varaibles

3.3.   Criterion Measures

At the initial and the final phase all the gymnasts completed questionnaires. Somatic & cognitive anxiety was evaluated by CASI-2 by Martin.

Psychological skills assessment scale was developed and standardized by Sharma and Sharma (2012) to test psychological skills among gymnasts. The detailed procedure for the development of the scale and exploratory analysis has been separately presented in chapter IV. Psychological Skills Assessment Scale for Gymnasts (PSAS-G), test the goal-setting, imagery, self-confidence, attention, motivation, arousal regulation and self-awareness of the gymnasts.

For the purpose of the training, a psychological skills training was prepared and administered for six weeks. Subject's logbook was also prepared by the research scholar, for the purpose of recording, assessing analyzing daily relaxation, goal-setting, self talk, imagery, attention and self-confidence. Federation of International Gymnastics code of points WAG and MAG, 2009-2012, was used to assess the pre and post Gymnastics performance of the subjects.

3.4.   Development of Training Program

An experimental Psychological Skills Training Program for six weeks (five days in a week), was developed for developing selected psychological skills such as Imagery, Relaxation, Confidence, Goal setting, Self-talk and Concentration for the Gymnasts. Before developing the training program the relevant literature was studied and different methods for developing the selected mental skills were studied. On the basis of their advantages over the other methods, were incorporated in the training. Scholar also considered the best suitable mental exercises for a gymnast while preparing the training schedule and placed in the training program. Since, training program was developed for each selected psychological skills each variable had its own training program including various exercises to have an impact on the gymnast's performance. Since, the training was carried for six weeks and the level of performance of the subjects was ranging from the state to the international level. Scholar has incorporated more than one technique so to break the monotonous factor as well as to ensure that the subjects would show interest in learning new things to enhance their psychological skills. Several exercises were incorporated in the training under various heads.

3.5. Administration of Training Program

The research scholar after making an approach to the various training Centre, choose to conduct her research program at Bhoir's Gymkhana in Dombivali, Mumbai as the owner of the Centre agreed to cooperate for training and had a sufficient number of gymnasts with participation at various levels from district to international level. The research scholar stayed at Dombivali for six weeks to apply the six weeks PST program on gymnasts, developed by the scholar. The developed training program was implemented in the following four stages:

Stage I–Rapport Development: The purpose of the initial meeting with the coaches and the gymnasts was to allow them to get acquainted with research scholar. And to provide valuable and unique insights of the mental skills to the gymnasts and coaches. Such small conversation helped scholar to create a rapport with players and coaches and ensured the friendly relation for an effective application of PST program.

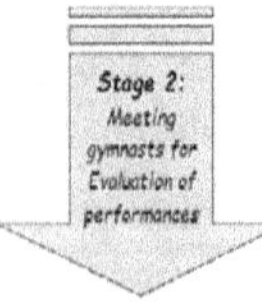

Stage II–Pre PST evaluation: The next stage involved determining the mental strengths and weaknesses of each gymnast. This was accomplished through a 30-40 minute meeting with the gymnasts. During this meeting, they were asked to complete the CSAI-2 and PSAS questionnaires. And the evaluation of their performances on various apparatuses was done by three judges on the basis of FIG, code of points, 2009.

Stage III–Psychological Skills Training: In the third stage, the scholar provided gymnasts with a six weeks psychological skills training. The PST sessions were conducted five days in a week to develop areas/factors limiting the athlete's present performance potential. The sessions lasted between 30 and 60 minutes. For each gymnast a separate handbook was prepared, which included a worksheet for all the activities they were executing during PST sessions, all the responses and actions by the gymnasts were filed in handbook. The PST session included an exercise from each variable everyday, which followed the sequence to start with relaxation followed by goal-setting, self-talk, imagery, attention and finally self-confidence exercises.

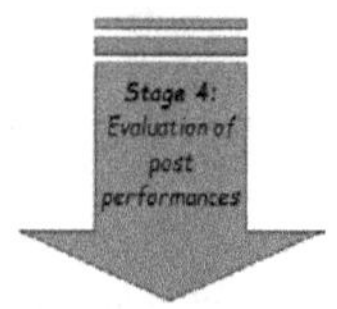

Stage IV–Application and Evaluation: PST program was applied on the gymnasts training for six weeks and the gymnasts developed an awareness of the Psychological Skills and began to practice the techniques or application of strategy under the guidance of the scholar and or the coach. Evaluation of the gymnasts performance was done at the two edges, first in the beginning before starting the PST Program and other after the completion of PST Program so that the assessment of the effect of Program on the gymnasts performance could be done, their routines on each apparatuses were evaluated by the three national qualified judges on the basis of FIG, code of points 2009. Schematic representation of the Administration of the program is presented in figure3.

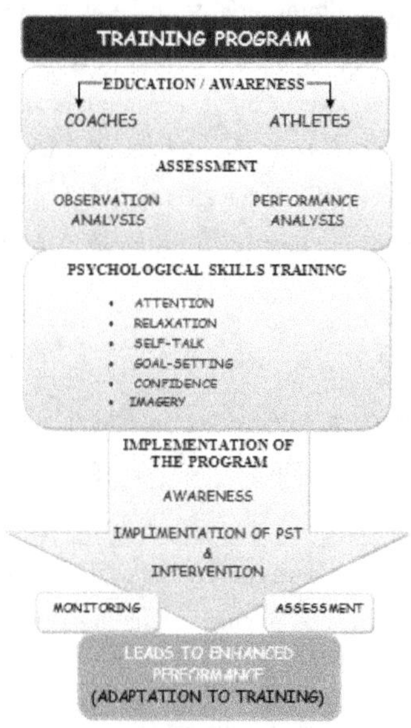

Figure 3: Schematic Representation of the Training Program

3.6.   Development of Logbook

Research scholar administered the training program for six weeks, five days a week. Total number of thirty sessions training was given to subjects.

To monitor the effectiveness of each session, scholar with consultation to the supervisor, designed a logbook of 20 pages for the purpose of the study, the front pages of the logbook included the demographic details of the gymnasts and other relevant information regarding the scholar and the research study. Followed by the consent letter, thoroughly read, understood and duly signed by all the gymnasts those who agreed to participate in the study voluntarily.

The worksheets of various variables were designed separately for each exercise to make it convenient for the gymnasts to respond and the research scholar could analyze them easily.

By designing logbook it was possible to collect the raw data of each subject separately for thirty days that is five days PST sessions in a week for six weeks PST program.

Though the psychological skills incorporated in the PST program were interrelated to each other, but a systematic sequence of order for the delivery of PST program was followed. Initially relaxation training was administered to make all the gymnasts feel fresh and stress free and function efficiently in setting the goals and further identify the negative thoughts and change them into positive ones, after positive self-talk and relaxed state of mind and body imagery training was planned followed by the attention training and at the end of the sessions self-confidence training was integrated in the PST, to provide gymnasts with a positive outlook at the end of the day, which may in turn benefit the gymnasts next day to enter the training center with more confidence and perform better.

3.7.   Collection of Data

In the present study data was collected as per the schedule in three phases from the regular trainee Gymnasts, selected as the subjects for the purpose of the study, from Bhoir's Gymkhana, Dombivali, Mumbai, India.

Scores of pre-test and post-test were collected to evaluate the effect of Psychological Skills Training program on the performance. Gymnasts took their pulse rate and respiratory rate by themselves.

Gymnasts initially were trained for three days to measure and calculate their pulse rate and respiratory rate.

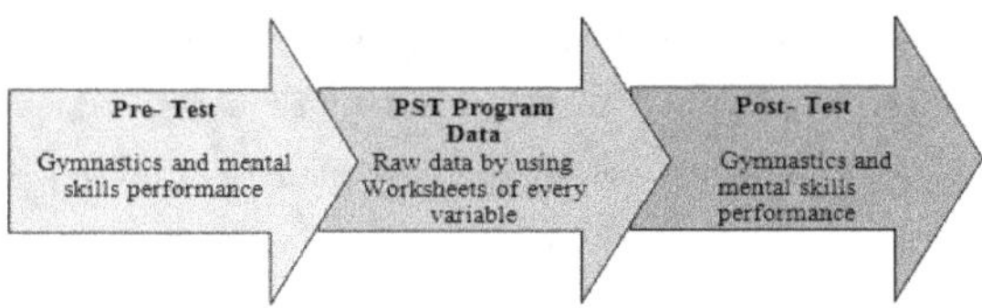

For the six variables, during PST program, every day the raw data was collected from every gymnast.

Relaxation: The data was collected every day before and after relaxation training, in the form of pulse, respiratory rate and tension level of the gymnasts. The gymnasts counted their own pulse and respiration rate on the command of scholar and marked themselves on the tension scale based on the present condition.

Goal-setting: The gymnasts used to set their technical and physical goals every Monday with a target date, after setting the goals, the gymnasts used to evaluate themselves on Friday to assess the percentage of success they have achieved throughout the week.

Self-talk: The gymnasts wrote their negative thoughts in the first two weeks of training. During the last four weeks gymnasts noticed their negative thoughts if any, and replaced them into positive thoughts. They also wrote the positive thoughts, which they had during the process of training.

Imagery: The gymnasts marked themselves on an imagery scale of five i.e no image present to Extremely Clear and Vivid Image for four statements measuring vividness, auditory, kinesthetic and mood of the gymnasts.

Attention: The data was collected from the scores of attention grid, mindfulness and shifting attention. The relevant cues were noticed by the gymnasts and used during the training.

Self-confidence: The gymnasts noted their doubtful and confident situation.

3.8. Procedure for the Assessment of Gymnastics Performance and Psychological Skills

Experiment Group	Pretest Performance &CSAI-2 and PSAS	PST Program + Gymnastics Training	Posttest Performance & CSAI-2 and PSAS
Control Group	Pretest Performance &CSAI-2 and PSAS	Gymnastics Training	Posttest Performance & CSAI-2 and PSAS
	Time: 1 Pre Test	Six Weeks	Time: 2 Post Test

Pretest Performance*:* Before starting the PST Program, the selected subjects were judged on the basis of FIG, code of points, 2009 by three qualified judges, and the research scholar herself also as one of the judges as scholar is an international qualified judge. Although, the evaluation in the gymnastics is subjective in nature but by using the FIG code of points, which has been formulated and developed in such a manner that the objectivity in judging was ensured to its optimum level.

CASI-2 by Martens, et al. (1990) was used to measure a somatic & cognitive anxiety and self-confidence of the gymnasts. Along with Psychological Skills Assessment Scale (PSAS) involves 29 items measuring seven mental skill, which are goal-setting, imagery, self-confidence, attention, motivation, psychic energy management and self-awareness, 5-point Likert scale is used, ranging from strongly disagree to strongly agree was completed by the gymnasts which helped the scholar to understand the weakness and the strengths of the gymnasts.

Posttest Performance: After completion of the PST Program the gymnast's performance was evaluated by qualified judges on the basis of the FIG, code of points, 2009. The CSAI-2 and PSAS-G were completed by the gymnasts.

Research scholar met gymnasts at their training complex for the pre and post Gymnastics and psychological skills performances of the gymnasts as was scheduled in the training program. The general scope of the study was explained to the gymnasts before starting the data collection. Emphasis was placed on the potential benefits deriving from the analysis of an individual's strategies, strengths, and weaknesses. The subjects were informed that their participation is voluntary and they were assured of the complete confidentiality and anonymity of their responses. All participants provided written consent and were then involved in the organized Questionnaire response sessions and gymnastics trial events at the two edges of the PST program lasted for six weeks.

Both the trials were conducted by the same individuals and the research scholar, who were trained and qualified FIG or GFI judges. The questionnaire response sessions was conducted by the research scholar herself, where all the instructions were clearly defined to the gymnasts, before starting filling the questionnaire responses.

3.9. Statistical Techniques

For the purpose of the present study since the data was collected from the different sources and require different treatment, therefore, different statistics was computed step wise in different sections.

Section I-Effect of PST on Psychological Skills

1) To analyze the effect of PST on the Psychological skills of the Gymnasts, descriptive statistics was employed with two ways ANOVA.

2) Further, in significant cases, test of simple effects in syntax of SPSS was further computed to test the interaction effect of trials with groups of training.

Section II-Effect of PST Program on the Performance of Various Gymnastics Apparatuses

1) To evaluate the effect of PST on the Gymnastics performance of the gymnasts, descriptive statistics was employed with One way ANCOVA.

2) Effect size was also computed to check the actual mean difference in the pre and post performance of the Gymnasts.

Section III-Correlation BETWEEN Gymnast's Performance and Psychological Skills

The Pearson product-moment correlation was run to determine the relationship between the Gymnast's performance and their psychological skills.

Section IV-Effect of Relaxation Training

To analyze the effect of relaxation training on the pulse, respiratory rate and tension level of the gymnasts, Repeated measure two way ANOVA was calculated, Further, the repeated measure within subjects was analyzed to check the linear trend by computing the data.

Section V-Effect of Imagery Training

To assess the effect of imagery training on the imagery ability of the gymnasts, Repeated measure ANOVA was calculated, Further, the repeated measure within subjects was analyzed to check the linear trend by computing the data.

Section VI-Attention Training

To analyze the effect of attention training, Repeated measure ANOVA was calculated, Further, the repeated measure within subjects was analyzed to check the linear trend by computing the data.

Section VII-Self-Talk and Goal-setting

Content analysis was employed in the assessment of self-talk and Goal-setting.

CHAPTER-4

DATA ANALYSIS

In the present experimental study data was collected from the Bhoir's Gymkhana, Dombivali, Mumbai, Gymnasts, a total number of fifty three Gymnasts, participated voluntarily and completed the study successfully. All gymnasts participated at least at the district/State/ national Gymnastics championships and some also represented India at international level. The age range of the subjects was between 9 to 17 years. The collected data was evaluated by applying various statistics based on the appropriateness of the data and objectives of the study. The analysis and results are divided into seven sections, each specified to each objective of the study. The results are presented in the tables and figures below, pertaining to their specific section.

4.1. Findings

The findings of the present study are presented in Section I to Section VII.

Section I-Effect of PST on Psychological Skills

Section- I: The objective was to test the effect of Psychological skill training on the Psychological skills of the Gymnasts. In the present study, a total of 53 male and female gymnasts completed the training program out of 60 initially selected Gymnasts. The gymnasts were selected and divided in to control and experimental groups, 29 subjects in experimental group (16 boys and 13 girls) and 24 in control group(12 boys and 12 girls).

To collect the data, subject's anxiety was measured by administering the CSAI-2 questionnaire and the psychological skills were measured by using PSAS developed by Sharma and Sharma, (2012), the data was collected at two stages, first, prior to the six weeks PST program and second, after administering the six weeks training, to examine the effect of PST on the Gymnast's psychological skills.

Psychological Skills within pre and post trials between experimental and control groups was analyzed by computing two way ANOVA to test the hypothesis. Two way ANOVA was computed with 2 X 2 factorial design, pre and post testing and experimental and control group division. Only interaction "f" value was considered in the present study. Test of simple effects in syntax of SPSS, was further computed to test the interaction effect of trials with groups of training. Since, the mean has increased from the pre data to the post data, the actual difference was computed by effect size. Researcher being sensitive to the distinction between statistical significance and practical significance added a step to the hypothesis testing by estimating the study's effect size. Estimate of effect size $[M_1-M_2/(SD_1+ SD_2/2)]$ (Huck, Schuyler W, 2012) could allow the researcher to talk about the pure strength of the measure, beyond saying simply that it is statistically significant or insignificant.

Section I, presents the findings on the effect of PST on psychological skills, the findings with regard to different psychological skills are presented in the table No.1 to table No.5.

Table 1: Descriptive Statistics of Total Psychological Skills Scores

Groups	Performance	Mean	Std. Deviation	N
Experimental	Pre	107.03	11.32	29
	Post	116.59	22.32	29
Control	Pre	104.00	13.03	24
	Post	103.50	14.58	24
Total	Pre	105.66	12.10	53
	Post	110.66	20.14	53

Table reveals the descriptive analysis of the total psychological skill scores before and after training between experimental and control group of selected sample. The tables represents the mean of pre test score in psychological skills of experimental group is 107.03 (SD 11.32) and post test scores of psychological skills is 116.59 (SD 22.32), Whereas, controlled group representing no significant change with pre test scores of psychological skills as 104.00, SD 13.03 and post psychological skills 103.50, SD 14.58.

Two way analysis was computed to find out the significant difference between pre and post psychological skills scores following training. The results are presented in table 2.

Table 2: Analysis of Two Way ANOVA of Psychological Skills within Pre and Post Trials between Experimental and Control Groups

Source	Sum of Squares	Df	Mean Square	F	P
Psychological Skills * groups	1330.36	1	1330.36	18.37	.00*

* $p< 0.01$.

The F test shows the significant difference at $p<0.01$ within pre and post trails between groups experimental and control.

It is evident from the table that a significant difference was found in the Psychological Skills with in pre and post trails between groups as F (Df=1, 51) 18.37, $p< 0.01$. It means the scores of Psychological Skills before and after training between experimental and control group differ significantly. So, interaction of trials with group does influence the psychological skills level of players. Thus, the null hypothesis that there is no significant influence of interaction on psychological skills is not accepted.

As f value is significant, test of simple effects in syntax of SPSS, was further computed to test the interaction effect of trials with groups of training. Findings are represented in table 3.

Table 3: Pairwise Comparisons Pre and Post Performances Among Experimental and Control Group Psychological Skills Performance

Performance	(I) Groups	(J) Groups	M D (I-J)	Std. Error	Sig.	95% Confidence Interval For Difference	
						Lower Bound	Upper Bound
Pre	Exp	Control	3.03	4.43	.49**	-5.76	11.83
	Control	Exp	-3.03	4.43	.49**	-11.83	5.76
Post	Exp	Control	13.08*	4.43	.00*	4.29	21.88
	Control	Exp	-13.08*	4.43	.00*	-21.88	-4.29

* p< 0.01, ** p> 0.05.

The table reveals that the pre performances of the experimental and control groups are similar as no significant difference was found (p, 0.49). However the difference between the post performances of the group was found significant with p< 0.01 indicating that the performance of the experimental group is statistically higher (M= 116.59) than the control group (M= 103.50).

The adjusted p-value for the comparisons of experimental and control groups (each for pre and post performance) is .05/2 = 0.03. By this criterion, the only difference, which is not, significant is pre performance between experimental and control group.

Further post hoc was computed, to check the difference between the pre and post trials of the experimental and controlled groups separately. Findings are presented in table 4.

Table 4: Pairwise Comparisons Among Experimental and Control Group for the Pre and Post Psychological Skills Performance

Groups	(I) Performance	(J) Performance	M D (I-J)	Std. Error	Sig.	95% Confidence Interval For Difference	
						Lower Bound	Upper Bound
Exp	Pre	Post	-9.55*	4.22	.02*	-17.92	-1.18
	Post	Pre	9.55*	4.22	.02*	1.18	17.92
Control	Pre	Post	.50	4.64	.91	-8.70	9.70
	Post	Pre	-.50	4.64	.91	-9.70	8.70

*p<0.05.

A significant difference was found in the pre and post performance of Psychological Skills within the experiment group as p<0.05, with no significant difference in the Psychological Skills pre and post trials of the control group with p> 0.05.

The adjusted p-value for the comparisons of pre and post performance (each for experimental and control groups) is .05/2 = 0.03. By this criterion, the only difference, which is not, significant, is control group between pre and post performance. The graphical representation of the results is presented in figure 1.

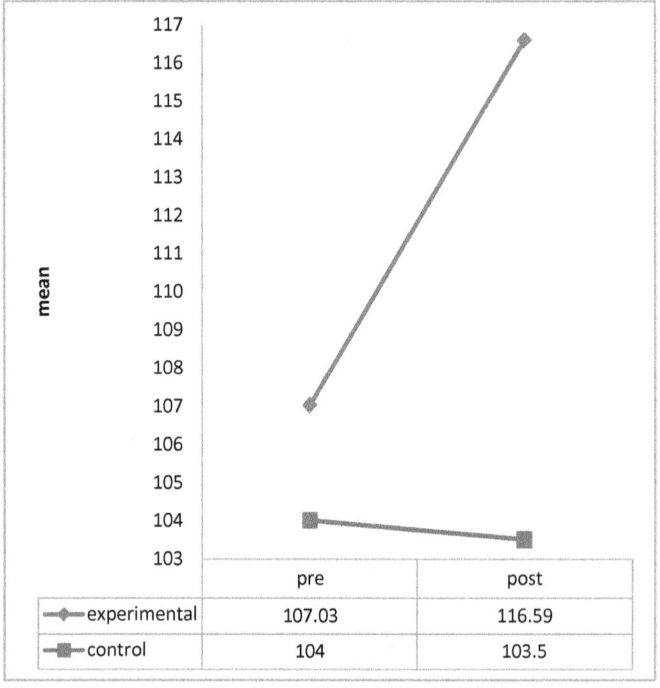

Figure 1: Graphical Representation of Experiment and Control Group's Pre and Post Psychological Skills Estimated Marginal Means

The graph represents the pre and the post psychological skills of experimental and control groups, it has been noticed that there is greater improvement in the psychological skills of the experimental group, while a little decline in the control group's psychological skills has been noticed. Descriptive Statistics with regard to Arousal Regulation was computed. The results are presented in table 5.

Table 5: Scores of Psychological Skills before Starting the PST and After the Completion of Six Weeks PST Program

S.No	Total PST		Arousal regulation		Goal setting		Self awareness		Imagery		Attention		Motivation		Self confidence	
	Pre	Post	Pre	Post	Pre	Post	Pre	Post	Pre	Post	Pre	Post	Pre	Post	Pre	Post
1	114	125	21	24	13	14	21	21	18	18	11	17	16	14	14	17
2	105	127	17	23	10	11	20	21	16	19	12	18	15	17	15	18
3	102	125	18	23	10	12	20	23	15	20	12	16	16	17	11	14
4	138	127	25	18	12	15	25	24	20	20	20	14	16	16	20	20
5	107	110	18	17	11	13	19	20	15	16	14	14	17	15	13	15
6	104	130	17	23	10	14	20	22	18	19	10	17	16	16	13	19
7	108	136	21	25	10	13	23	23	17	20	10	18	15	18	12	19
8	98	99	17	16	11	10	20	21	14	17	12	11	13	13	11	11
9	100	109	19	19	12	13	15	17	14	17	11	12	16	17	13	14
10	105	120	16	22	11	11	20	19	16	19	12	15	15	17	15	17
11	122	135	20	25	14	13	22	22	17	20	13	17	19	19	17	19
12	111	121	19	20	12	12	21	19	19	20	10	16	16	17	14	17
13	110	108	18	17	15	11	22	19	16	15	11	16	16	14	12	16
14	113	119	19	20	12	13	22	20	14	17	14	17	15	15	17	17
15	93	119	19	19	12	12	13	23	9	18	12	16	15	15	13	16
16	121	134	19	22	12	14	18	24	17	20	17	16	20	19	18	19
17	105	120	16	20	12	11	21	23	16	18	12	14	15	18	13	16
18	103	106	17	20	11	10	20	18	17	15	9	13	15	15	14	15
19	95	125	18	24	9	12	17	20	13	18	12	16	13	17	13	18
20	121	123	20	24	14	13	21	22	16	17	18	16	15	15	17	16
21	97	105	16	21	12	13	15	22	13	13	10	9	18	16	13	11
22	93	98	14	16	11	9	18	16	13	15	9	10	16	18	12	14
23	106	128	16	22	9	12	19	22	14	18	14	18	15	20	19	16
24	85	134	11	25	10	15	18	20	13	18	6	20	18	18	9	18
25	129	132	21	24	14	14	22	24	19	20	16	16	17	14	20	20
26	107	127	19	22	10	13	17	22	15	18	14	14	18	19	14	19
27	107	97	15	14	12	11	23	17	17	16	15	10	15	.16	10	13

Note:	low	Average	High	Very High

The table indicates the pre and post score of PST assessment of all the Gymnasts those who participated in the training program for six weeks. The training program composite six psychological skills namely, Goal-setting, attention, Self-awareness, arousal regulation, imagery and self-confidence. It is evident from the table that most of the Gymnasts had scored high in the pre Psychological Skills assessment and some of the gymnast scored average in arousal regulation, self-awareness and attention, while the post Psychological Skills assessment shows very high scores of the Gymnasts.

Psychological skills of the Gymnasts highlighted with yellow colour Indicates low scores, however Gymnasts have improved from average to high and very high are indicated with green and brown colour respectively. Comparing pre and post scores, an improvement in the psychological skills of the Gymnasts has been observed.

Section II-Effect of PST Program on the Performance of Gymnasts

Section II- presents the results with regard the effect of PST program on the performance of the gymnasts on various apparatus, in the present study 53 Gymnasts (male and female) participated, There were 29 subjects in experimental group (16 boys and 13 girls), and 24 subjects in control group (12 boys and 12 girls). The Gymnasts in experimental group were provided with the PST for six weeks and were evaluated to check the effect of PST on performance. Their performance on each apparatus was evaluated at two stages i.e prior to the PST and after completion of the training.

One-Way ANCOVA was computed with pre performance covariated (to remove the effects of performance prior to the PST imparted) as the subjects were unequally distributed among the groups, Further the mean difference between experimental and control groups were analyzed by pairwise comparison, level of significance was set at 0.05. The findings with regard to different apparatuses are presented in the tables below.

Statistical analysis has shown that the data is statistically insignificant, however the post test mean is greater than the pre test mean. In the present study, beyond statistical significance, the findings appeared of considerable practical significance.

As, gymnastics is a game in which the code of points is designed in such a way that the difficulty level (values ranging from 0.10 to 0.70) and the execution of the gymnasts are evaluated by providing the score in points (sum of 0.10, 0.20 etc) i.e score improves with 0.10, 0.20 etc. so even the minute change in the scores of the gymnasts is a big achievement because to learn a new skill higher with a value of 0.10 in difficulty level, take months of practice.

Since, statistically insignificance was obtained between means, although the mean has increased from the pre data to the post data, the actual difference was computed by effect size. Researcher being sensitive to the distinction between statistical significance and practical significance added a step to the hypothesis testing by estimating the study's effect size. Estimate of effect size $[M_1\text{-}M_2/(SD_1 + SD_2/2)]$ (Huck, Schuyler W, 2012) could allow the researcher to talk about the pure strength of the measure, beyond saying simply that it is statistically significant or insignificant. In the following section, only group's results have been presented in the results of between subjects effect, as effect between experimental and control groups has to be checked.

Effect of PST on the Performance of the Indian Boys Gymnasts

Performance was measured by adding the scores on all the apparatuses i.e six apparatuses for boys and four apparatuses for girls. The descriptive statistics was computed on Boys all-around performance and the results are given in the table 6.

Table 6: Descriptive Statistics of Experimental and Control Group on Boys All Around

Groups	Experimental Group	Control Group
Adjusted Mean	32.90	31.47

Table reflects the mean value of the post performance of experimental group higher (32.90) as compare to lower performance (31.47) of the control group.

One way ANCOVA was computed on all around performance of Boys. The result is presented in the table 7.

Table 7: Analysis of One Way ANCOVA of All Around Boys Performance Within Pre and Post Trials between Experimental and Control Groups

Source of Variance	Df	SS	MSS	F	p
Groups (Experimental and Control)	1	10.88	10.88	1.07	.31*

*p>0.05.

a. R Squared = .974 (Adjusted R Squared = .972)

The above table shows the One-Way ANCOVA calculations, showing that there is an insignificant difference in post performance among groups as obtained F = 1.07 at p > 0.05. It means that the adjusted mean scores of post performance in players of experimental and control group do not differ significantly. So, there is no group influence on the performance of players. Thus, the null hypothesis that there would be no significant influence of group on performance of players when pre performance of control and experimental group is considered as covariate, is accepted. The graphical presentation of the post performances of the experimental and control groups are presented in figure 2.

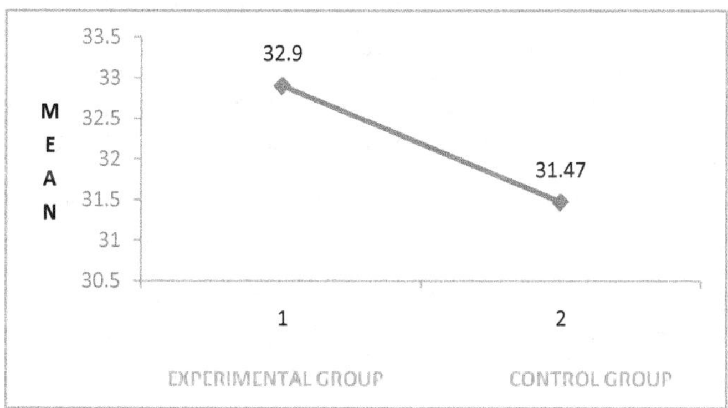

Figure 2: Graphical Representation of Experiment and Control Group's Post Performance Estimated Marginal Means

The graph clearly represents, when pre performance being equal (covariated), the post performance of experimental group is higher (32.9) when compared to the performance of control group (31.47). Statistically the difference is insignificant but due to PST intervention, the improvement in the performance of experimental group is greater than the improvement in performance of control group in the absence of the PST training. To check the actual difference in the post performances of the experimental and control group, the effect size was computed, which is 0.75, which falls in the category of high difference in the performance.

Effect of PST on the Performance of the Girls

Since the girl's apparatus are different from the boys, the effect of PST was also studied on All-around performance and presented from table No. 8 to 10.

Table 8: Descriptive Statistics of Experimental and Control Group All Around Performance of Girls

Groups	Experimental Group	Control Group
Adjusted Mean	24.16	19.45

Table reflects the mean value of the post performance of experimental group higher (24.16) as compare to lower performance (19.45) of the control group. One way ANCOVA was and the result is presented in the table 9.

Table 9: Analysis of One way ANCOVA of Girl'sAll Around Performance within Pre and Post Trials between Experimental and Control Groups

Source of Variance	Df	SS	MSS	F	p
Groups (Experimental and Control)	1	84.00	84.00	5.28	.03*

*p<0.05, a. R Squared = .933 (Adjusted R Squared = .927)

The above table shows the One-Way ANCOVA calculations, showing that there is significant difference in post performance among groups as obtained F = 5.28 at p< 0.05.

It means that the adjusted mean scores of post performance in players of experimental and control group differ significantly. So, there is group influence on the performance of players.

Thus, the null hypothesis that there is no significant influence of group on performance of players when pre performance of control and experimental group is considered as covariate, is not accepted.

Further the mean difference between experimental and control group were analyzed by computing the data. The finding is presented in table 10.

Table 10: Pairwise Comparisons of Post Adjusted Group Mean for All Around Performance Among Experimental and Control Group

(I) Group	(J) Group	M D (I-J)	Std. Error	Sig.	95% Confidence Interval For Difference	
					Lower Bound	Upper Bound
Exp	Cont	4.70*	2.04	.03*	.45	8.95

*p<0.05.

The above table exhibits that the mean difference among Experimental and Controlled group is 4.70, which is significant at p < 0.05. Graphical representation is given in figure 3.

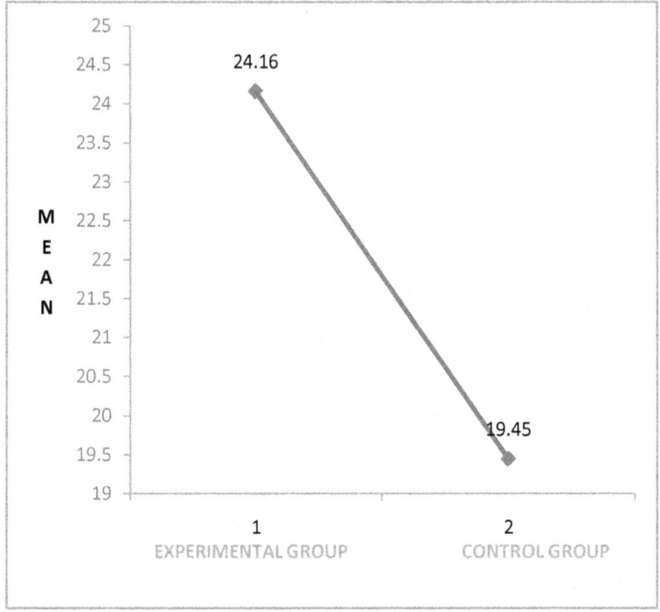

Figure 3: Graphical Representation of Experiment and Control Group's Post Performance of all Around Performance Estimated Marginal Means

The graph clearly represents that when pre performance being equal, the post performance of experimental group is higher (24.16) when compared to the performance of control group (19.45). Statistically also the difference is significant. PST intervention's effect on, the improvement in the performance of experimental group was tested by computing effect size. Therefore, to check the actual difference in the means effect size was computed, and the effect size is 1.13, which represents the high difference.

Section III-Correlation between Gymnast's Performance and their Psychological Skills

In the present section, The Pearson product-moment correlation was run to determine the relationship between the gymnast's performance and their psychological skills level of the Gymnasts. The data was collected after the successful completion of six weeks Psychological Skills training program, the scores of performance on various apparatuses were also recorded and psychological skills were measured and recorded by using PSAS for the purpose of evaluation. The results are presented in the table No.11 and table No. 12.

Table 11: Pearson Correlation Coefficient between Psychological Skills and Performance on Various Apparatuses of Male Gymnasts

Psychological skills	Performance on Apparatuses						
	Vault Table	Floor Exercise	High Bar	Parallel Bars	Pommel Horse	Roman Rings	Total Performance
Arousal	.32	.16	.38*	.41*	.39*	.34	.39*
Goal Setting	.46*	.28	.36	.37	.28	.33	.40*
Imagery	.40*	.29	.43*	.52**	.55**	.45*	.51**
Attention	.25	.31	.37	.38	.26	.31	.37
Motivation	.26	.06	.29	.29	.34	.21	.28
Self Awareness	.03	-.01	.18	.25	.24	.15	.16
Self Confidence	.38*	.13	.47*	.46*	.51**	.47*	.46*
Total Psy. Skills	.35	.20	.43*	.47*	.45*	.40*	.44*

** p< 0.01, *p<0.05.

The results of Pearson product-moment correlation reveals that a significant positive relationship exist between arousal and high bar, parallel bars, pommel horse and the total performance of the boys as r (25) = 0.38, 0.41, 0.39 and 0.39 respectively, p< 0.05. Whereas the arousal regulation is insignificantly related with Vault table, floor exercise and Roman rings as r (25) = 0.32, 0.16 and 0.34 respectively, p> 0.05. The Goal-setting is correlated with the performance on Vault table and with total performance scores (r (25) = 0.46 and 0.40 respectively, p< 0.05), but not correlated with floor exercise, high bar, parallel bars, pommel horse and roman rings as r (25) = 0.28, 0.36, 0.37, 0.28 and 0.33 respectively, p> 0.05. Imagery represents a significant positive relation with the performance on Vault table, High bar and

Roman Rings r (25) = 0.40, 0.43 and 0.45 respectively, p< 0.05, and Imagery is highly correlated with Parallel Bars, Pommel Horse and overall performance scores at r (25) = 0.52, 0.55 and 0.51 respectively, p< 0.01. Whereas, Imagery is not correlated with Floor exercise performance as obtained r is 0.29, p> 0.05. Self-confidence is correlated with Vault Table, High Bar, Parallel Bars, Roman Rings and Total performance scores as r (25) = 0.38, 0.47, 0.46, 0.47 and 0.46 respectively, p< 0.05 and positively correlated with Pommel Horse as r (25) = 0.51, p< 0.01 and not correlated with floor exercise performance as r = 0.13, p> 0.05. The total Psychological Skills performance of the Gymnasts are significantly positively related with the performance on High Bar, Parallel Bars, Pommel Horse, Roman Rings and overall performance on all the apparatuses at (r (25) = 0.43, 0.47, 0.45, 0.40 and 0.44 respectively, p< 0.05). Whereas insignificantly correlated with vault table and floor exercise performance as r (25) = 0.35 and 0.20 respectively, p> 0.05.

Moreover, the variables Attention, Motivation, Self-awareness and performance on Floor exercise are not correlated with any of the variables.

Table 12: Pearson Correlation Coefficient between Psychological Skills and Performance on Various Apparatuses of Female Gymnasts

Psychological Skills	Performance on Apparatuses				
	Vault Table	Floor Exercise	Uneven Bars	Balancing Beam	Total Performance
Arousal Regulation	.37	.44*	.50*	.46*	.48*
Goal Setting	-.06	.19	.17	.05	.07
Imagery	.25	.26	.41*	.48*	.39
Attention	.38	.62**	.49*	.47*	.52**
Motivation	-.03	.14	.12	.09	.07
Self Awareness	.20	.51**	.29	.41*	.36
Self Confidence	.42*	.48*	.56**	.56**	.55**
Total Psy. Skills	.29	.50*	.47*	.48*	.46*

** p< 0.01, *p<0.05.

The Pearson product-moment correlation was run to determine the relationship between the female Gymnast's performance and their psychological skills. The results reveals that a significant positive relationship exist between arousal regulation and Floor exercise, uneven bars, balancing beam and the overall performance of female gymnasts as r (23) = 0.44, 0.50, 0.46 and 0.48 respectively, p< 0.05. Whereas arousal regulation is not significantly related with

Vault table as r (23) = 0.32, p> 0.05. Imagery represents a significant positive relation with the performance on uneven bars, balancing beam and total performance scores r (23) = 0.41, 0.48 and 0.39 respectively, p< 0.05, Whereas, Imagery is not significantly correlated with vault table and Floor exercise performance as r 0.25 and 0.26 respectively, p> 0.05. Attention is correlated with uneven bars and balancing beam as r = .49 and .47 respectively, p < .05, whereas highly correlated with floor exercise and overall performance scores as r (23)=.62 and .52 respectively, p< .01, but does not correlate significantly with the performance on vault table. Self awareness is significantly correlated with floor exercise and balancing beam performance as r = .51, p< .01 and r = .41, p< .05 respectively, whereas no correlation exist with vault table, uneven bars and overall performance scores as r 0.20, 0.29 and 0.36 respectively, p> 0.05. Self-confidence is correlated with Vault Table and floor exercise performance scores as r (23) = 0.42 and 0.48 respectively, p< 0.05 and highly positive correlated with uneven bars, balancing beam and total performance scores as r (23) = 0.56, 0.56 and 0.55 respectively, p< 0.01. The total Psychological Skills performance of the Gymnasts are significantly positively related with the performance on floor exercise, uneven Bars, balancing beam and overall performance on all the apparatuses at r (23) = 0.50, 0.47, 0.48, and 0.46 respectively, p< 0.05. Whereas insignificantly correlated with vault table performance as r (23) = 0.29, p> 0.05. Moreover, the variable Motivation is not significantly correlated with any of the variables.

Section IV-Effect of Relaxation Training

One of the objectives of the study was to test the effectiveness of the each training session of Relaxation training program on the Gymnasts. The gymnasts in experimental group were provided relaxation training using various techniques for thirty days. Thirty sessions, altogether could not be analyzed due to the systems limitations. Therefore, analyses was made weekly by computing the repeated measure design for each week. To analyze each week's relaxation training effect, the data of every Friday was used. Predata was collected each day before starting the training program and post data after the training was provided, the data was collected for the purpose of the analyses.

Effect of relaxation training was studied by employing repeated measure design. Three parameters were recorded and evaluated i.e pulse, Respiratory rate and tension level. Findings with regard to pulse are presented from tableNo.13 to 15, results pertaining to respiratory rate are presented from table no. 16 to table no. 18 whereas results pertaining to tension level are presented from table no.19 to table no.21.

Effect of Relaxation Training on the Pulse Rate

Table 13: Descriptive Statistics of Pulse Rate for Six Weeks' Relaxation Training Sessions

Groups	Pulse	Mean	Std. Deviation	N
Day 1 (Pre)	Pre	42.56	7.58	16
	Post	37.38	6.49	16
Week 1	Pre	44.25	5.29	16
	Post	39.38	7.32	16
Week 2	Pre	42.69	5.82	16
	Post	37.82	6.29	16
Week 3	Pre	46.75	4.88	16
	Post	41.19	4.10	16
Week 4	Pre	47.44	5.03	16
	Post	42.38	4.13	16
Week 5	Pre	45.62	4.66	16
	Post	39.62	7.02	16
Week 6	Pre	46.50	4.98	16
	Post	41.63	5.70	16

Table reveals the descriptive analysis of the pulse rate before and after relaxation training between pre and 6 weeks sessions of selected sample. The tables represents the mean of day 1 pre pulse 42.56 (SD 7.58) and post 37.38 (SD 6.49), week 1 pre pulse 44.25 (SD 5.29) and post 39.38 (SD 7.32), week 2 pre pulse 42.69 (SD 5.82) and post 37.82 (SD 6.29), week 3 pre pulse 46.75 (SD 4.88) and post 41.19 (SD 4.10), week 4 pre pulse 47.44 (SD 5.03) and post 42.38 (SD 4.13), week 5 pre pulse 45.62 (SD 4.66) and post 39.62 (SD 7.02)and week 6 pre pulse 46.50 (SD 4.98) and post 41.63 (SD 5.70).

To test the sphericity assumption Mauchly's test was computed, the results are presented in the table 14.

Table 14: Mauchly's Test

Within Subjects Effect	Mauchly's W	X^2	Df	Sig.	Epsilon		
					Greenhouse-Geisser	Huynh-Feldt	Lower-bound
Days * Pulse	.12	26.64	20	.16*	.64	.89	.17

*p>0.05.

Table reveals that the Mauchly's test for interaction of Days * Pulse does not significantly violate the sphericity assumption because the significant value is greater than 0.05, W= .12, X^2 = 26.64, p> .05, ε < .75, Therefore, we have used Epsilon Greenhouse-Geisser to adjust f score and the conservative Epsilon should be used to adjust the df as recommended by Girden, E. R. (1992).

Further F test was computed to check the difference at 0.05 within pre and post trails between the six weeks sessions and the f was computed by considering the Epsilon of Greenhouse-Geisser adjusted.

Table 15: Summary of Two Way ANOVA of Pulse Rate within Pre and Post Trials between Six Weeks Sessions

Source		SS	Df	MS	F	P
Pulse * groups	Greenhouse-Geisser	8.86	6	1.47	.16	.99*
(pre & post)	Error	813.29	57.67	14.10		

*p>0.05.

The F test shows the insignificant difference at 0.05 within pre and post trails between six weeks sessions. It is evident from the table that an insignificant difference was found in the Pulse with in pre and post trails between six weeks sessions as Greenhouse-Geisser adjusted F (Df = 6, 90) .16, p> 0.05. It reflects that the rate of pulse before and after training between sessions do not differ significantly.

Since, between the weeks, no significant difference was obtained, each week's pre and post pulse rate has been presented graphically to understand the trend of decrease in the pulse rate. The graphical representation of data is presented in figure 4.

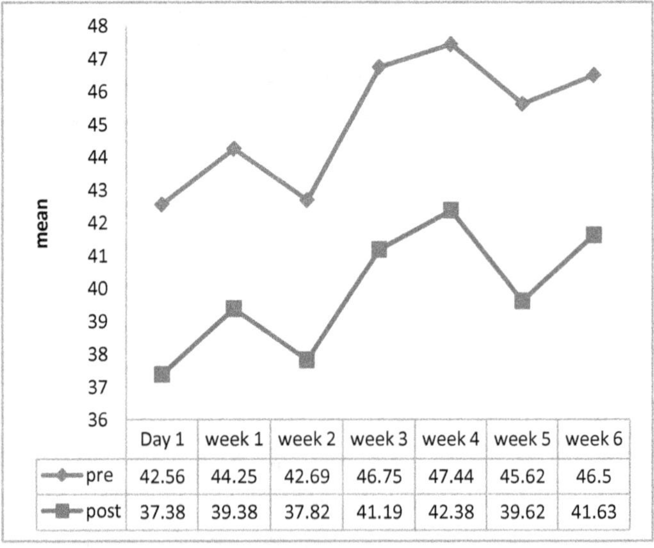

Figure 4: Graphical Representation of Pre and Post Pulse Means of Six Weeks Sessions

The graphical representation shows the pre and post pulse rate of the gymnasts during six weeks relaxation training. The graph clearly state that in each week the pulse rate prior to the relaxation training is greater than the pulse rate immediately after relaxation training, through this it can be analyzed that the relaxation training was effective in each week to decrease the pulse rate and bring the gymnasts in much relaxed state.

To throw more light on the trend of changes in the pulse rate, effect size [M1- M2/(SD1 + SD2/2)] was calculated to understand the actual difference between the pre and post pulse rate of the Gymnasts, Pre has moderate effect size at 0.74, week 1, week 2,week 3, week 4, week 5 and week 6 have large effect size with 0.77, 0.80, 1.24, 1.10, 1.03 and 0.91 respectively.

To understand the actual change in the pulse rate of the gymnasts after each relaxation training session, the repeated measure has been computed for all the five sessions within each week, the results are presented in the tables below.

Effect of Relaxation Training on the Respiratory Rate of the Gymnasts

To assess the effectiveness of each relaxation session on the respiration rate of the gymnasts, subjects respiratory rate before and after each relaxation session was recorded and analyzed. The results are presented in the given tables below.

Table 16: Descriptive Statistics of Respiratory Rate Six Weeks Relaxation Training Sessions

Groups	Respiratory rate	Mean	Std. Deviation	N
Day 1	Pre	20.37	4.57	16
	Post	17.37	4.76	16
Week 1	Pre	18.12	4.06	16
	Post	16.25	3.36	16
Week 2	Pre	18.94	4.58	16
	Post	16.00	2.97	16
Week 3	Pre	19.69	3.70	16
	Post	16.00	4.00	16
Week 4	Pre	18.44	3.10	16
	Post	15.12	2.19	16
Week 5	Pre	19.19	2.59	16
	Post	15.56	2.97	16
Week 6	Pre	18.56	3.71	16
	Post	14.56	2.06	16

Table reveals the descriptive analysis of the respiratory rate scores before and after relaxation training between pre and 6 weeks sessions of selected sample. The tables represents the mean of day 1 pre respiratory rate 20.37 (SD 4.57) and post 17.37 (SD 4.76), week 1 pre respiratory rate 18.12 (SD 4.06) and post 16.25 (SD 3.36), week 2 pre respiratory rate 18.94 (SD 4.58) and post 16.00 (SD 2.97), week 3 pre respiratory rate 19.69 (SD 3.70) and post 16.00 (SD 4.00), week 4 pre respiratory rate 18.44 (SD 3.10) and post 15.12 (SD 2.19), week 5 pre respiratory rate 19.19 (SD 2.59) and post 15.56 (SD 2.97) and week 6 pre respiratory rate 18.56 (SD 3.71) and post 14.56 (SD 2.06) high mean effect size 1.39.

Is there significant difference among the six weeks scores, repeated measure was computed and the results are presented in the table 17.

Table 17: Mauchly's Test

Within Subjects Effect	Mauchly's W	X^2	Df	Sig.	Epsilon		
					Greenhouse-Geisser	Huynh-Feldt	Lower-bound
Days * Respiratory rate	.14	25.02	20	.21*	.62	.84	.17

*p>0.05.

Table reveals that the Mauchly's test for interaction of Days * Respiratory Rate does not significantly violate the sphericity assumption because the significant value is greater than 0.05, W= .14, X^2 = 25.02, p> .05. ε < .75, therefore, we have used Epsilon Greenhouse-Geisser to adjust f score and the conservative Epsilon should be used to adjust the df as recommended by Girden, E. R. (1992).

Further F test was computed to check the difference at 0.05 within pre and post trails between the sessions of six weeks and the f was computed by considering the Epsilon of Greenhouse-Geisser adjusted.

Table 18: Summary of Two Way ANOVA of Respiratory Rate within Pre and Post Trials between Six Weeks Sessions

Source		SS	Df	MS	F	P
Respiratory rate * groups	Greenhouse-Geisser	23.48	6	3.91	1.68	.14*
(pre & post)	Error	209.52	55.50	3.77		

*p>0.05.

It is evident from the table that an insignificant difference was found in the Respiratory rate with in pre and post trails between six weeks sessions as F (Df = 6, 90) 1.68, p> 0.05. It reflects that the scores of respiratory rate before and after training between sessions do not differ significantly.

Since, between the days, no significant difference was obtained, each day's pre and post respiratory rate has been presented graphically in figure 5to understand the trend of decrease in the respiratory rate after the completion of each relaxation training session.

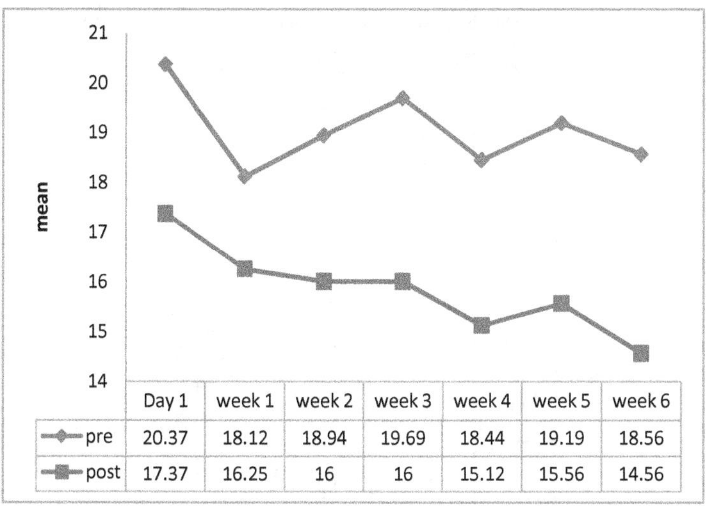

	Day 1	week 1	week 2	week 3	week 4	week 5	week 6
pre	20.37	18.12	18.94	19.69	18.44	19.19	18.56
post	17.37	16.25	16	16	15.12	15.56	14.56

Figure 5: Graphical Representation of Pre and Post Respiratory Rate Means of Six Weeks Sessions

The graphical representation shows the pre and post respiration rate of the gymnasts during six week's relaxation training. The graph clearly state that each week, the respiration prior to the relaxation training is greater than the respiration rate immediately after relaxation training, through this it can be analyzed that the relaxation training was effective each week to drop down the respiration rate and bring the gymnasts in much relaxed state.

As statistical insignificant difference was obtained but through graph the decrease in respiratory rate could be observed, to understand the actual difference between the pre and post respiratory rate of the Gymnasts, effect size [M1- M2/ (SD1 + SD2/ 2)] was calculated, pre, week 1 and week 2 have moderate effect size at 0.64,0.50, 0.78 respectively with large mean effect size in week 3, week 4, week 5 and week 6 with effect size 0.96, 1.25, 1.31 and 1.39 respectively.

Effect of Relaxation Training on the Tension Level of the Gymnasts

The scholar had also recorded the level of tension before and after imparting each relaxation training session, to understand how tense subjects were before following the training sessions and how calm they felt after each session. The subjects state of tense and calmness was measured in 1 to 8 scale where 1 is indicating calmness and the 8 is indicating tension. Findings are presented from the table No. 19 to No. 21.

Table 19: Descriptive Statistics of Tense Six Weeks Relaxation Training Sessions

Groups	Tense	Mean	Std. Deviation	N
Day 1	Pre	4.31	1.89	16
	Post	2.56	1.50	16
Week 1	Pre	3.93	1.73	16
	Post	2.12	1.14	16
Week 2	Pre	4.37	1.63	16
	Post	2.31	1.19	16
Week 3	Pre	4.62	2.12	16
	Post	2.69	2.12	16
Week 4	Pre	4.12	1.75	16
	Post	2.00	1.15	16
Week 5	Pre	3.93	1.61	16
	Post	2.06	1.39	16
Week 6	Pre	4.31	1.54	16
	Post	2.12	1.20	16

Table reveals the descriptive analysis of the tense scores before and after relaxation training between pre and 6 weeks sessions of selected sample.

The tables represents the mean of day 1 pre tense 4.31 (SD 1.89) and post 2.56 (SD 1.50), week 1 pre tense 3.93 (SD 1.73) and post 2.12 (SD 1.14), week 2 pre tense 4.37 (SD 1.63) and post 2.31 (SD 1.19), week 3 pre tense 4.62 (SD 3.70) and post 2.69 (SD 2.12), week 4 pre tense 4.12 (SD 1.75) and post 2.00 (SD 1.15), week 5 pre tense 3.93 (SD 1.61) and post 2.06 (SD 1.39) and week 6 pre tense 4.31 (SD 1.54) and post 2.12 (SD 1.20).

Test of Mauchly's was computed to check the difference at 0.05 within pre and post trails between six week's sessions.

Table 20: Mauchly's Test

Within Subjects Effect	Mauchly's W	X^2	Df	Sig.	Epsilon		
					Greenhouse-Geisser	Huynh-Feldt	Lower-bound
Days * Tense	.03	44.59	20	.00*	.48	.61	.17

*p<0.01.

Table reveals that the Mauchly's test for interaction of Days * Respiratory Rate significantly violate the sphericity assumption because the significant value is less than 0.01, W= .03, X^2 = 44.59, p< .01.

But Greenhouse-Geisser is less than 0.75. Therefore, the f value, for the main effect of treatment does not need to be corrected for violations of sphericity.

Further F test was computed by considering the Epsilon of Greenhouse-Geisser adjusted to check the difference at 0.05 within pre and post trails between the sessions of six weeks.

Table 21: Summary of Twoway ANOVA of Tense Rate within Pre and Post Trials between Six Weeks Sessions

Source	Greenhouse-Geisser	SS	Df	MS	F	P
Tense * groups (pre & post)		1.30	2.89	.45	.35	.78*
	Error	55.55	43.29	1.28		

*p>0.05.

The F test shows the insignificant difference at 0.05 within pre and post trails between six weeks sessions. An insignificant difference was found in the Tense with in pre and post trails between six weeks sessions as F (Df = 2.89, 90) .35, p> 0.05.

It reflects that the scores of tense before and after training between sessions do not differ significantly.

Since, between the days, no significant difference was obtained, each day's pre and post tension level has been presented graphically in figure 42 to understand the trend of decrease in the tension level after the completion of each relaxation training session.

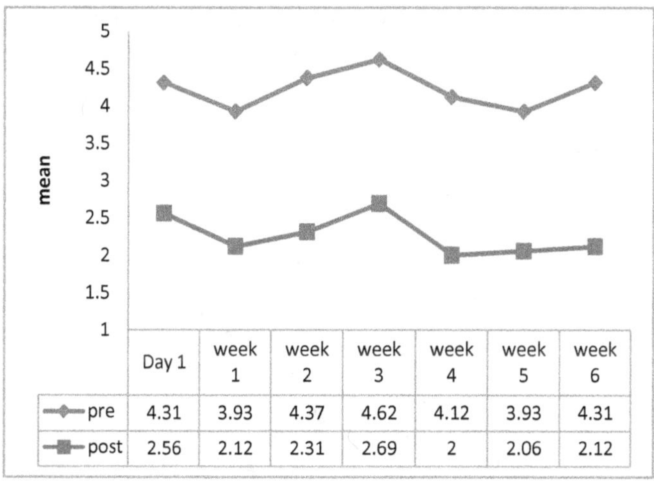

Figure 6: Graphical Representation of Pre and Post Tense Means of Six Weeks Sessions

The graphical representation shows the pre and post tension rate of the gymnasts during six week's relaxation training. The graph clearly state that in each week, the tension level prior to the relaxation training is greater than the tension level immediately after relaxation training, through this it can be analyzed that the relaxation training was effective each day of every week to reduce the tension level of the gymnasts and bring them in a more calm state.

As statistical insignificant difference was obtained but through graph the decrease in tension level could be observed, to understand the actual difference between the pre and post tension level of the Gymnasts, effect size [M1- M2/(SD1 + SD2/2)] was calculated, Day 1 (pre), week 1, week 2, week 3, week 4, week 5 and week 6 have large effect size with 1.03, 1.26, 1.46, 0.91, 1.46, 1.25 and 1.60 respectively.

Section V-Effect of Imagery Training

Although, imagery training is influential to bring about the desirous changes in an athlete's performance. However, the learning process of imagery is such that it is difficult to assess whether the subjects are involved in imagery or not as its always a mental picture in your brain that you imagine, nobody else is able to see what you imagine in your brain. To have a better evaluation of how clearly the subjects are able to visualize the different important aspect of imagery, the Scholar every day, after rendering the imagery sessions, had collected the feedback using a four statement questionnaire on the four important areas i.e kinesthetic, auditory, vividness and mood. To assess the effectiveness of each training session, repeated measure was computed. Since, all the thirty sessions could not be computed due to software's limitations, the analysis was done on the weekly basis. The results are presented from table No. 22 to table No. 41.

Imagery Using Kinesthetic

Table 22: Descriptive Statistics of Kinesthetic Imagery Training Sessions for Six Weeks

Week 1	Mean	S D	N
Pre (Day 1)	4.15	.87	20
Week 1	4.40	.68	20
Week 2	4.40	.59	20
Week 3	4.70	.57	20
Week 4	4.70	.57	20
Week 5	4.70	.57	20
Week 6	4.75	.55	20

The descriptive statistics table reveals the mean and the standard deviation of Imagery with kinesthetic sessions over the six weeks training, i.e first session represents the least value with the improvement in the imagery with kinesthetic training scores by the last week of the training.

Numerical representation of the data, day 1 (M, 4.15 ± .87), Week 1 (M, 4.40 ± .68), Week 2 (M, 4.40 ± .59), week 3 (M, 4.70 ± .57), week 4 (M, 4.70 ± .57), week 5 (M, 4.70 ± .57) and in week 6 (M= 4.75 ± .55).mean effect size of pre and week 6 is high at 0.84.

Test of sphericity was computed to test if there is a significant difference among the six week's scores, and the results are presented in the table below.

Table 23: Mauchly's Test

Within Subjects Effect	Mauchly's W	X^2	Df	Sig.	Epsilon		
					Greenhouse-Geisser	Huynh-Feldt	Lower-bound
Kinesthetic Imagery six weeks Training	.18	28.94	20	.09*	.68	.88	.17

*p>0.05.

Mauchly's test for six weeks Kinesthetic Imagery Training, reveals that there is no significant violation of the sphericity assumption because the significant value is greater than 0.05, W= .18, X^2 = 28.94, p> .05. Ɛ < .75,

Therefore, we have used Epsilon Greenhouse-Geisser to adjust f score and the conservative Epsilon should be used to adjust the df as recommended by Girden, E. R. (1992).

Further F test was computed by considering the Epsilon of Greenhouse-Geisser adjusted to check the difference at 0.05 within pre and post trails between the sessions of six weeks.

Table 24: Repeated Measure ANOVA for Comparison of Means During Six Weeks of Kinesthetic Imagery Training

Source		SS	Df	MS	F	P
Kinesthetic Imagery	Greenhouse-Geisser	6.24	6	1.04	3.32	.00*
(Six Weeks)	Error	35.76	77.45	.46		

*p<0.01.

The above table shows the repeated measure ANOVA calculations, showing that there is significant improvement in the scores of Imagery with kinesthetic during the six weeks training as obtained F = 3.32 at p<0.01. It means that ability to imagine using kinesthetic in players has developed significantly.

So, there is a influence of Imagery Training on the kinesthetic ability of the Gymnasts. Thus, the null hypothesis that there is no significant influence of training, is not accepted.

Further, the repeated measure within subjects was analyzed to check the linear trend by computing the data. The finding is presented in the table below.

Table 25: Repeated Measure within Subject Analysis for Six Weeks Sessions of Kinesthetic Imagery

Source of Variance		SS	df	MSS	F	p
Six Weeks Sessions	Linear	5.21	1	5.21	11.07	.00*
	Quadratic	.61	1	.61	3.03	.09
	Cubic	3.79	1	3.79	.00	1.00
Error (six week sessions)	Linear	8.94	19	.47		
	Quadratic	3.82	19	.20		
	Cubic	5.33	19	.28		

*p< 0.01.

There is significant linear effect of training f (1, 19) = 11.07 p< 0.01. It can be concluded that six weeks imagery training had a linear effect of improvement in the imagery using kinesthetic.

So, the number of sessions in six weeks could improve the imagery with kinesthetic significantly.

The pairwise comparisons for the main effect of training corrected, using a bonferroni adjustment was further computed.

Table 26: Pairwise Comparisons Among Six Week Sessions of Kinesthetic Imagery Training

(I) Group	(J) Group	MD (I-J)	Std. Error	Sig.	95% Confidence Interval For Difference	
					Lower Bound	Upper Bound
Pre (Day 1)	Week 1	-.25	.20	.23	-.68	.18
	Week 2	-.25	.20	.23	-.68	.18
	Week 3	-.55*	.18	.01**	-.94	-.16
	Week 4	-.55*	.23	.03*	-1.04	-.06
	Week 5	-.55*	.19	.01**	-.96	-.13
	Week 6	-.60*	.23	.02*	-1.1	-.11
Week 1	Week 2	.00	.19	1.00	-.40	.40
	Week 3	-.30	.16	.08	-.64	.04
	Week 4	-.30	.16	.08	-.64	.04
	Week 5	-.30	.19	.14	-.70	.10
	Week 6	-.35*	.13	.01**	-.62	-.07
Week 2	Week 3	-.30	.16	.08	-.64	.04
	Week 4	-.30	.16	.08	-.64	.04
	Week 5	-.30	.16	.08	-.64	.04
	Week 6	-.35*	.17	.05*	-.70	-.00
Week 3	Week 4	.00	.14	1.00	-.30	.30
	Week 5	.00	.18	1.00	-.37	.37
	Week 6	-.05	.13	.72	-.33	.23
Week 4	Week 5	.00	.18	1.00	-.37	.37
	Week 6	-.05	.08	.58	-.23	.13
Week 5	Week 6	-.05	.17	.77	-.40	.30

** p< 0.01, *p<0.05.

"The table indicates that the main effect reflects a significant difference p< .05 between pre (day 1) and week, 3 week 4, week 5 and week 6 at p< 0.05 and difference of week 1 and week 2 with week 6 is p< 0.05."The graphical representation of the mean values of pre data and six weeks, kinesthetic imagery sessions is presented in the figure 7.

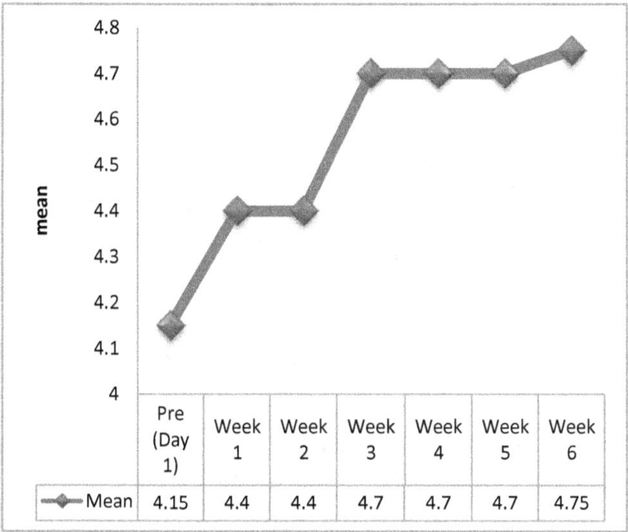

Mean	Pre (Day 1)	Week 1	Week 2	Week 3	Week 4	Week 5	Week 6
Mean	4.15	4.4	4.4	4.7	4.7	4.7	4.75

Figure 7: Graphical Representation of Mean Values of Six Weeks Kinesthetic Imagery Training

The graphical representation of the mean values of six weeks depicts a significant linear development in the Kinesthetic Imagery Training.

Further, to test the effectiveness of each session, week wise calculations were done for six weeks for each session i.e five sessions each week, to assess the each session's change during the week training.

Imagery Training Using Mood

Table 27: Descriptive Statistics of Mood Imagery Training Sessions for Six Weeks

Week 1	Mean	S D	N
Pre (Day 1)	4.05	1.05	20
Week 1	4.05	.82	20
Week 2	4.45	.60	20
Week 3	4.50	.83	20
Week 4	4.35	.74	20
Week 5	4.30	.57	20
Week 6	4.75	.44	20

The descriptive statistics table reveals the mean and the standard deviation of Mood Imagery sessions over the six weeks training, i.e first session represents the least value with the improvement in the mood imagery training scores by the last week of the training. Numerical representation of the data, day 1 (M, 4.05 ± 1.05), Week 1 (M, 4.05 ± .82), Week 2 (M, 4.45 ± .60), week 3 (M, 4.50 ± .83), week 4 (M, 4.35 ± .74), week 5 (M, 4.30 ± .57) and in week 6 (M= 4.75 ± .44).

Table 28: Mauchly's Test

Within Subjects Effect	Mauchly's W	X^2	Df	Sig.	Epsilon		
					Greenhouse-Geisser	Huynh-Feldt	Lower-bound
Mood Imagery six weeks Training	.09	39.82	20	.01*	.61	.78	.17

*p<0.01.

Table reveals that the Mauchly's test indicated that assumption of sphericity have been violated, X^2 (20) = 39.82, p< .01. ε < .75,

Therefore, we have used Epsilon Greenhouse-Geisser to adjust f score and the conservative Epsilon should be used to adjust the df as recommended by Girden, E. R. (1992).

To test if there significant difference among the week's scores of imagery using mood, repeated measure was computed and the results are presented in the table below.

Table 29: Repeated Measure ANOVA for Comparison of Means During Six Weeks of Mood Imagery Training

Source		SS	Df	MS	F	P
Mood Imagery	Greenhouse-Geisser	5.96	3.60	1.66	3.22	.02*
	Error	51.36	69.99	.73		

*p<0.05.

The above table shows the repeated measure ANOVA calculations, showing that there is significant improvement in the scores of Mood Imagery during the six weeks training as obtained F = 3.22 at p < 0.05. It means that ability to imagine using mood in players has developed significantly. So, there is influence of Imagery Training. Thus, the null hypothesis that there is no significant influence of training, is not accepted.

The pairwise comparisons for the main effect of training corrected, using a bonferroni adjustment was further computed.

Table 30: Pairwise Comparisons Among Six Week Sessions of Mood Imagery Training

(I) Group	(J) Group	M D (I-J)	Std. Error	Sig.	95% Confidence Interval For Difference	
					Lower Bound	Upper Bound
Pre (Day 1)	Week 1	.00	.24	1.00	-.84	.84
	Week 2	-.40	.21	1.00	-1.14	.34
	Week 3	-.45	.27	1.00	-1.38	.48
	Week 4	-.30	.27	1.00	-1.25	.65
	Week 5	-.25	.28	1.00	-1.23	.73
	Week 6	-.70	.25	.25	-1.58	.18
Week 1	Week 2	-.40	.197	1.00	-1.09	.29
	Week 3	-.45	.256	1.00	-1.35	.45
	Week 4	-.30	.252	1.00	-1.18	.58
	Week 5	-.25	.176	1.00	-.87	.37
	Week 6	-.70*	.164	.01**	-1.27	-.13
Week 2	Week 3	-.05	.23	1.00	-.87	.77
	Week 4	.10	.16	1.00	-.46	.66
	Week 5	.15	.19	1.00	-.53	.83
	Week 6	-.30	.18	1.00	-.93	.33
Week 3	Week 4	.15	.17	1.00	-.43	.73
	Week 5	.20	.19	1.00	-.45	.85
	Week 6	-.25	.20	1.00	-.96	.46
Week 4	Week 5	.05	.17	1.00	-.54	.64
	Week 6	-.40	.18	.88	-1.04	.24
Week 5	Week 6	-.45*	.11	.02*	-.85	-.05

** p< 0.01, *p<0.05.

"The table indicates that the main effect reflects a significant difference p< .05 between week 1 and week 6, week 5 and week 6 at p< 0.01 and p< 0.05 respectively."

Further, the repeated measure within subjects was analyzed to check the linear trend by computing the data. The finding is presented in the table below.

Table 31: Repeated Measure within Subject Analysis for Six Weeks Sessions of Mood Imagery

"Source of Variance"		SS	df	MSS	F	p
Six Weeks Sessions	Linear	4.46	1	4.46	5.78	.03*
	Quadratic	.04	1	.04	.07	.79
	Cubic	1.01	1	1.01	3.29	.09
Error	Linear	14.68	19	.77		
	Quadratic	9.91	19	.52		
	Cubic	5.82	19	.31		

*p<0.05.

There is significant main linear effect of training f (1, 19) = 5.78 p< 0.05. It can be concluded that six weeks imagery training had a linear effect of improvement in the mood imagery. So, the number of sessions in six weeks could improve the mood imagery significantly. The graphical representation of the mean values of pre and six weeks, mood imagery's five sessions is presented below.

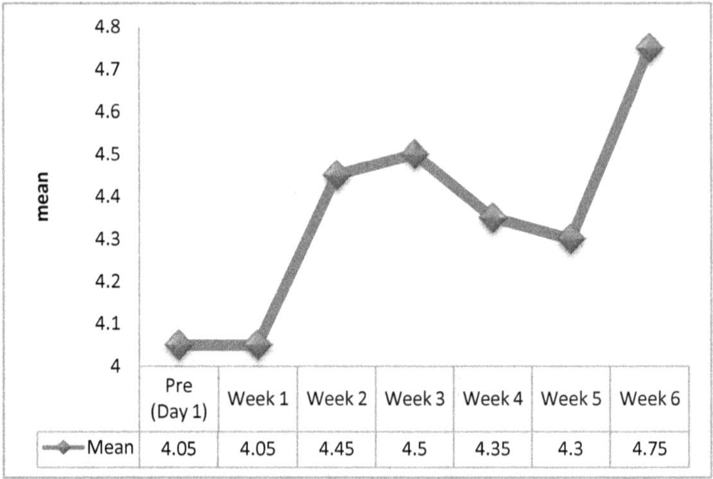

Figure 8: Graphical Representation of Mean Values of Six Weeks Mood Imagery Training

The graphical representation of the mean value of six weeks depicts a significant linear development in the Imagery using mood. It could be understood that imagery training using mood was effective over the period of six weeks.

Further calculations are week wise i.e first week to sixth week's scores were calculated, to assess each session's change during that particular week training.

Imagery Using Auditory

Auditory imagery involves the visualization of the picture or the scene with full effect of sound, it includes the realization of all the sounds of the scene imagined to have the feeling of real execution.

Table 32: Descriptive Statistics of Auditory Imagery Training Sessions for Six Weeks

Week 1	Mean	S D	N
Pre (Day 1)	3.20	1.28	20
Week 1	4.20	.89	20
Week 2	4.50	.69	20
Week 3	4.50	.69	20
Week 4	4.60	.68	20
Week 5	4.30	.73	20
Week 6	4.65	.49	20

The descriptive statistics table reveals the mean and the standard deviation of Auditory Imagery sessions over the six weeks training, i.e first session represents the least value with the improvement in the auditory imagery training scores by the last week of the training. Numerical representation of the data, day 1 (M, 3.20 ± 1.28), Week 1 (M, 4.20 ± .89), Week 2 (M, 4.50 ± .69), week 3 (M, 4.50 ± .69), week 4 (M, 4.60 ± .68), week 5 (M, 4.30 ± .73) and in week 6 (M= 4.65 ± .49).

Test of sphericity was computed to test the significant difference among the week's scores, and the results are presented in the table below.

Table 33: Mauchly's Test

Within Subjects Effect	Mauchly's W	X^2	Df	Sig.	Epsilon		
					Greenhouse-Geisser	Huynh-Feldt	Lower-bound
Auditory Imagery six weeks	.25	23.18	20	.29*	.68	.88	.17

*p>0.05.

Table reveals that the main effect of training does not significantly violate the sphericity assumption because the significant value is greater than 0.05, W= .25, X^2 = 23.18, p> .05."Ɛ < .75, Therefore, we have used Epsilon Greenhouse-Geisser to adjust f score and the conservative Epsilon should be used to adjust the df as recommended by Girden, E. R. (1992).

Repeated Measure ANOVA test was computed to check the difference at 0.05 between the sessions of six weeks.

Table 34: Repeated Measure ANOVA for Comparison of Means During Six Weeks of Auditory Imagery Training

Source		SS	Df	MS	F	P
Auditory Imagery	Greenhouse-Geisser	30.18	6	5.03	10.17	.00*
	Error	56.39	77.17	.73		

*p<0.01.

The above table shows the repeated measure ANOVA calculations, showing that there is significant improvement in the scores of Auditory Imagery during the six weeks training as obtained F = 10.17 at p < 0.01. It means that ability to imagine using auditory in players has developed significantly. So, there is influence of Imagery Training. Thus, the null hypothesis that there is no significant influence of training, is not accepted.

The pair wise comparisons for the main effect of training corrected, using a bonferroni adjustment was further computed.

Table 35: Pairwise Comparisons Among Six Weeks Sessions of Auditory Imagery Training

(I) Group	(J) Group	M D (I-J)	Std. Error	Sig.	95% Confidence Interval For Difference	
					Lower Bound	Upper Bound
Pre (Day 1)	Week 1	-1.00*	.25	.02*	-1.88	-.12
	Week 2	-1.30*	.25	.00**	-2.18	-.42
	Week 3	-1.30*	.32	.01**	-2.41	-.19
	Week 4	-1.40*	.25	.00**	-2.29	-.50
	Week 5	-1.10*	.29	.03*	-2.14	-.05
	Week 6	-1.45*	.23	.00**	-2.27	-.63
Week 1	Week 2	-.30	.19	1.00	-.98	.38
	Week 3	-.30	.23	1.00	-1.11	.51
	Week 4	-.40	.22	1.00	-1.18	.38
	Week 5	-.10	.20	1.00	-.81	.61
	Week 6	-.45	.18	.52	-1.09	.19
Week 2	Week 3	.00	.19	1.00	-.67	.67
	Week 4	-.10	.20	1.00	-.81	.61
	Week 5	.20	.22	1.00	-.59	.99
	Week 6	-.15	.18	1.00	-.79	.49
Week 3	Week 4	-.10	.24	1.00	-.94	.74
	Week 5	.20	.17	1.00	-.40	.80
	Week 6	-.15	.17	1.00	-.73	.43
Week 4	Week 5	.30	.23	1.00	-.51	1.11
	Week 6	-.05	.18	1.00	-.69	.59
Week 5	Week 6	-.35	.15	.65	-.87	.17

** p< 0.01, *p<0.05.

The table "indicates that the main effect reflects a significant difference p< .05 between pre (day) and week 1, week 2, week 3, week, week 5 and week 6 at p< 0.01."

Further, the repeated measure within subjects was analyzed to check the linear, quadratic and Cubic trend by computing the data. The finding is presented in the table below.

Table 36: Repeated Measure within Subject Analysis for Six Weeks Sessions of Auditory Imagery

Source of Variance		SS	Df	MSS	F	p
Six Weeks Sessions	Linear	15.45	1	15.45	22.79	.00*
	Quadratic	8.71	1	8.72	13.95	.00*
	Cubic	5.21	1	5.21	14.22	.00*
Error (six week sessions)	Linear	12.88	19	.68		
	Quadratic	11.87	19	.62		
	Cubic	6.96	19	.37		

*p< 0.01.

There is significant linear effect of training f (1, 19) = 22.79 p< 0.01. It can be concluded that six weeks imagery training had a linear effect of improvement in the auditory imagery. So, the number of sessions in six weeks could improve the auditory imagery significantly.

The graphical representation of the mean values of six weeks auditory imagery sessions is presented in the given figure 9.

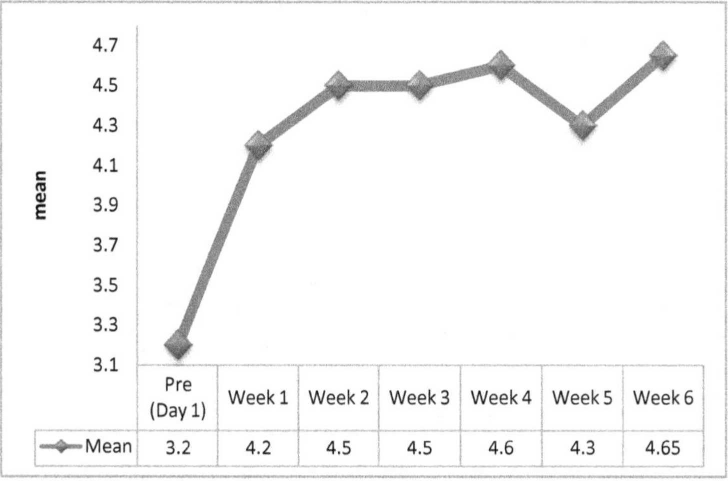

Figure 9: Graphical Representation of Mean Values of Six Weeks Auditory Imagery Training

The graphical representation of the mean values of six weeks depicts a significant linear, quadratic and cubic development in the Auditory Imagery Training.

Further calculations were done for each week i.e. first week to sixth week, to assess the each session's change during a particular week's training.

Imagery Training Using Vividness

Imagery training's most important aspect is to imagine the image with very clarity and noticing each and every thing in the image happening vividly, to check if gymnasts could imagine the situation vividly, following calculations were done, the results are presented in the tables below.

Table 37: Descriptive Statistics of Vivid Imagery Training Sessions for Six Weeks

Week 1	Mean	S D	N
Pre (Day 1)	4.30	.66	20
Week 1	4.55	.76	20
Week 2	4.70	.57	20
Week 3	4.85	.37	20
Week 4	4.85	.37	20
Week 5	4.85	.37	20
Week 6	4.95	.22	20

The descriptive statistics table reveals the mean and the standard deviation of Vivid Imagery sessions over the six weeks training, i.e first session represents the least value with the improvement in the vivid imagery training scores by the last week of the training. Numerical representation of the data, day 1 (M, 4.30 ± .66), Week 1 (M, 4.55 ± .76), Week 2 (M, 4.70 ± .57), week 3 (M, 4.85 ± .37), week 4 (M, 4.85 ± .37), week 5 (M, 4.85 ± .37) and in week 6 (M= 4.95 ± .22).

Test of sphericity was computed to test the significant difference among the day's scores, and the results are presented in the table below.

Table 38: Mauchly's Test

Within Subjects Effect	Mauchly's W	X^2	Df	Sig.	Epsilon		
					Greenhouse-Geisser	Huynh-Feldt	Lower-bound
Vivid Imagery six weeks	.17	29.31	20	.08*	.62	.78	.17

*p>0.05.

Table reveals that "the main effect of training does not significantly violate the sphericity assumption because the significant value is greater than 0.05, W= .17, X^2 = 29.31, p> .05."Ɛ < .75, Therefore, we have used Epsilon Greenhouse-Geisser to adjust f score and the conservative Epsilon should be used to adjust the df as recommended by Girden, E. R. (1992).

Further F test was computed to check the difference at 0.05 between the sessions of six weeks.

Table 39: Repeated Measure ANOVA for Comparison of Means during Six Weeks of Vivid Imagery Training

Source		SS	Df	MS	F	P
Vivid Imagery	Greenhouse-Geisser	6.19	6	1.03	4.99	.00*
	Error	16.46	61.83	.27		

*p<0.01.

The above table shows the repeated measure ANOVA calculations, showing that there is significant improvement in the scores of Vivid Imagery during the six weeks training as obtained F = 4.99 at p<0.01. It means that ability to imagine vividly in players has developed significantly. So, it shows that there is an influence of Imagery Training. Thus, the null hypothesis that there is no significant influence of training, is not accepted.

The pairwise comparisons for the main effect of training corrected, using a bonferroni adjustment was further computed.

Table 40: Pairwise Comparisons Among Six Week Sessions of Vivid Imagery Training

(I) Group	(J) Group	M D (I-J)	Std. Error	Sig.	95% Confidence Interval For Difference	
					Lower Bound	Upper Bound
Pre (Day 1)	Week 1	-.25	.22	1.0	-1.00	.51
	Week 2	-.40	.17	.59	-.99	.19
	Week 3	-.55	.18	.16	-1.19	.09
	Week 4	-.55*	.15	.04*	-1.09	-.01
	Week 5	-.55*	.13	.01**	-1.02	-.08
	Week 6	-.65*	.15	.00**	-1.17	-.12
Week 1	Week 2	-.15	.13	1.00	-.61	.31
	Week 3	-.30	.18	1.00	-.93	.33
	Week 4	-.30	.16	1.00	-.87	.27
	Week 5	-.30	.18	1.00	-.93	.33
	Week 6	-.40	.15	.35	-.93	.13
Week 2	Week 3	-.15	.13	1.00	-.61	.31
	Week 4	-.15	.11	1.00	-.53	.23
	Week 5	-.15	.13	1.00	-.61	.31
	Week 6	-.25	.12	1.00	-.68	.18
Week 3	Week 4	.00	.10	1.00	-.36	.36
	Week 5	.00	.13	1.00	-.44	.44
	Week 6	-.10	.10	1.00	-.45	.25
Week 4	Week 5	.00	.10	1.00	-.36	.36
	Week 6	-.10	.10	1.00	-.45	.25
Week 5	Week 6	-.10	.10	1.00	-.45	.25

** p< 0.01, *p<0.05.

"The table indicates that the main effect reflects a significant difference p< .05 between week 4 and week 5 and week 6 at p< 0.01."

Further, the repeated measure within subjects was analyzed to check the linear trend by computing the data. The finding is presented in the table below.

Table 41: Repeated Measure Within Subject Analysis for Six Weeks Sessions of Vivid Imagery

"Source of Variance"		SS	Df	MSS	F	P
Six Weeks Sessions	Linear	5.21	1	5.21	25.60	.00**
	Quadratic	.77	1	.77	3.13	.09*
	Cubic	.13	1	.13	.41	.53*
Error (six week sessions)	Linear	3.864	19	.20		
	Quadratic	4.68	19	.25		
	Cubic	6.20	19	.33		

** p< 0.01, *p>0.05.

There is significant main effect of training f (1, 19) = 25.60 p< 0.01. It can be concluded that six weeks imagery training had a linear effect of improvement in the vivid imagery. So, the number of sessions in six weeks could improve the vivid imagery significantly.

The graphical representation of the mean values of six weeks vivid imagery session is presented in the table below.

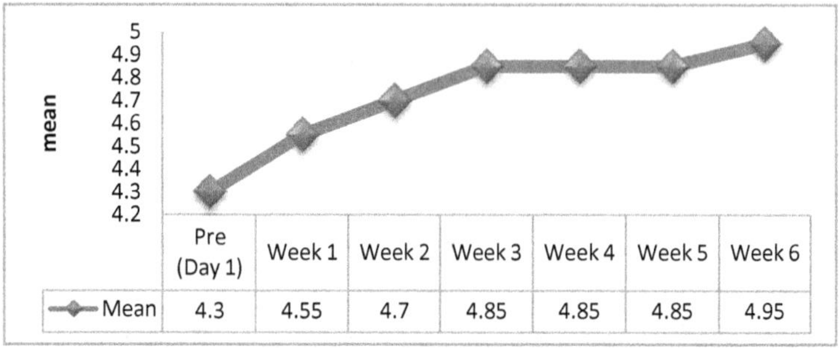

Figure 10: Graphical Representation of Mean Values of Six Weeks Vivid Imagery Training

The graphical representation of the mean values of six weeks imagery training, depicts a linear development in the Vivid Imagery scores.

Further calculations were done for each week i.e week 1 to week 6, to assess the effect of each session in a particular week, the results of each week are presented separately in the tables below.

Section VI–Effect of Attention Training

As attention is essential for performing one's best, the experimental group subjects were imparted training to improve their attentional skills. For developing the attention ability of the Gymnasts, the scholar had chosen various techniques i.e Attention grid for first two weeks, relevant cues for next two weeks and lastly shifting attention for the last two weeks. All the three methods were incorporated in the program, the data collected from the subjects in each session for attention grid exercise were recorded by the scholar for the purpose of evaluation and the relevant cues were also analyzed qualitatively.

For evaluating the effect of attention training, Repeated measure ANOVA was calculated, Further, the repeated measure within subjects was analyzed to check the trend by computing the data and for analyzing relevant cues, qualitative content analysis was executed.

Attention Grid

The subjects respond to the attention grid for the first two weeks, the subjects followed the instructions of the scholar and practiced the attention grid for improving the attention ability. The descriptive statistics and repeated measure were applied, the findings are presented from table no. 42 to table No. 47.

Table 42: Descriptive Statistics of Attention Training Sessions using Attention Grid for Two Weeks

Days	Mean	S D	N
Day 1	6.58	2.72	24
Day 2	7.12	2.88	24
Day 3	7.12	3.25	24
Day 4	8.00	3.71	24
Day 5	7.08	2.78	24
Day 6	11.25	3.54	24
Day 7	7.08	3.29	24
Day 8	10.96	3.25	24
Day 9	8.58	3.06	24
Day 10	12.71	4.79	24

The descriptive statistics table reveals the mean and the standard deviation of Attention grid sessions over the two weeks training of attention, i.e first session represents the least value with the improvement in the attention grid scores by the last week of the training. Numerical representation of the data, day 1 (M, 6.58 ± 2.72), day 2 (M, 7.12 ± 2.88), day 3 (M, 7.12 ± 3.25), day 4 (M, 8. ± 3.71), day 5 (M, 7.08 ± 2.78), day 6 (M, 11.25 ± 3.54) day 7 (M= 7.08 ± 3.29), day 8 (M, 10.96 ± 3.25), day 9 (M, 8.58 ± 3.06) and day 10 (M, 12.71 ± 4.79).

To test if there is a significant difference among the attention grid sessions' scores, repeated measure was computed and the results are presented in the table below.

Table 43: Mauchly's Test

Within Subjects Effect	Mauchly's W	X^2	Df	Sig.	Epsilon		
					Greenhouse-Geisser	Huynh-Feldt	Lower-bound
Attention grid two weeks Training	.24	28.23	44	.97*	.73	1.00	.11

*p>0.05.

Table reveals that "the main effect of training does not significantly violate the sphericity assumption because the significant value is greater than 0.05, W= .24, X^2 = 28.23, p> .05."ε < .75, Therefore, we have used Epsilon Greenhouse-Geisser to adjust f score and the conservative Epsilon should be used to adjust the df as recommended by Girden, E. R. (1992). Further F test was computed by considering the Epsilon of Greenhouse-Geisser adjusted to check the difference at 0.05 between the attention grid sessions for ten days.

Table 44: Repeated Measure ANOVA for Comparison of Means During Two Weeks of Attention grid Training

Source	Greenhouse-Geisser	SS	Df	MS	F	P
Attention grid		1027.60	9	114.18	14.65	.00*
	Error	1613.60	151.64	10.64		

*p<0.01.

The above table shows the repeated measure ANOVA calculations, showing that there is significant improvement in the scores of Attention grid during the two weeks training as obtained F = 14.65 at p < 0.01. It means that ability of attention using attention grid in players has developed significantly. So, there is influence of attention Training.

Thus, the null hypothesis that there is no significant influence of attention grid training, is not accepted. The pairwise comparisons for the main effect of training corrected, using a bonferroni adjustment was further computed. The result is presented in the table below.

Table 45: Pairwise Comparisons Among Two Week's Sessions of Attention GridTraining

(I) Group	(J) Group	M D (I-J)	Std. Error	Sig.	95% Confidence Interval For Difference	
					Lower Bound	Upper Bound
Day 1	Day 2	-.54	.67	1.00	-3.05	1.96
	Day 3	-.54	.65	1.00	-2.97	1.88
	Day 4	-1.42	.678	1.00	-3.94	1.11
	Day 5	-.50	.65	1.00	-2.91	1.91
	Day 6	-4.67*	.78	.00**	-7.58	-1.75
	Day 7	-.50	.79	1.00	-3.45	2.45
	Day 8	-4.37*	.73	.00**	-7.12	-1.63
	Day 9	-2.00	.75	.65	-4.82	.82
	Day 10	-6.12*	.99	.00**	-9.84	-2.40
Day 2	Day 3	.00	.71	1.00	-2.66	2.66
	Day 4	-.87	.83	1.00	-3.97	2.23
	Day 5	.04	.77	1.00	-2.82	2.91
	Day 6	-4.12*	.76	.00**	-6.95	-1.29
	Day 7	.04	.76	1.00	-2.79	2.87
	Day 8	-3.83*	.71	.00**	-6.47	-1.19
	Day 9	-1.46	.82	1.00	-4.54	1.62
	Day 10	-5.58*	.92	.00**	-9.03	-2.13
Day 3	Day 4	-.87	.68	1.00	-3.42	1.67
	Day 5	.04	.58	1.00	-2.14	2.22
	Day 6	-4.12*	.83	.00**	-7.23	-1.02
	Day 7	.04	.70	1.00	-2.58	2.66
	Day 8	-3.83*	.66	.00**	-6.30	-1.36
	Day 9	-1.46	.79	1.00	-4.39	1.48
	Day 10	-5.58*	.85	.00**	-8.75	-2.42
Day 4	Day 5	.92	.75	1.00	-1.87	3.71
	Day 6	-3.25	.91	.08	-6.66	.16
	Day 7	.92	.80	1.00	-2.07	3.89
	Day 8	-2.96*	.75	.03*	-5.75	-.16
	Day 9	-.58	.92	1.00	-3.99	2.83
	Day 10	-4.71*	.93	.00**	-8.18	-1.231
Day 5	Day 6	-4.17*	.73	.00**	-6.88	-1.45
	Day 7	.00	.75	1.00	-2.80	2.80
	Day 8	-3.87*	.62	.00**	-6.19	-1.56
	Day 9	-1.50	.68	1.00	-4.02	1.02
	Day 10	-5.62*	.99	.00**	-9.31	-1.93

Table 45 continue: Pairwise Comparisons Among Two Week's Sessions of Attention GridTraining

(I) Group	(J) Group	M D (I-J)	Std. Error	Sig.	95% Confidence Interval For Difference	
					Lower Bound	Upper Bound
Day 6	Day 7	4.17*	.83	.00**	1.07	7.26
	Day 8	.29	.77	1.00	-2.56	3.15
	Day 9	2.67	.81	.14	-.35	5.69
	Day 10	-1.46	1.15	1.00	-5.73	2.82
Day 7	Day 8	-3.87*	.73	.00**	-6.59	-1.15
	Day 9	-1.50	.77	1.00	-4.37	1.37
	Day 10	-5.62*	1.03	.00**	-9.45	-1.79
Day 8	Day 9	2.37	.66	.07	-.10	4.85
	Day 10	-1.75	1.00	1.00	-5.48	1.98
Day 9	Day 10	-4.12*	1.11	.05*	-8.24	-.01

** p< 0.01, *p<0.05.

The table "indicates that the main effect reflects a significant difference" p< .05 of day 1, day 2 and day 3 with day 6, day 8 and day 10. Difference of day 4 and day 5 with day 8 & day 10.Difference between day 6 and day 7.Significant difference between day 7 and day 8, day 10. Day 9 is significantly different with day 10 at p< 0.05.

Further, the repeated measure within subjects was analyzed to check the linear trend by computing the data. The finding is presented in the table below.

Table 46: Repeated Measure within Subject Analysis for Two Weeks Sessions of Attention Grid Training

Source of Variance		SS	Df	MSS	F	P
Two Weeks Sessions	Linear	536.85	1	536.85	63.34	.00**
	Quadratic	20.04	1	20.04	2.11	.16*
	Cubic	18.39	1	18.39	1.69	.21*
Error (Two weeks sessions)	Linear	194.93	23	8.47		
	Quadratic	218.68	23	9.51		
	Cubic	250.31	23	10.88		

** p< 0.01, *p>0.05.

There is significant main linear effect of training f (1, 23) = 63.34 p< 0.01. Quadratic effect insignificant at p< 0.05. It can be concluded that two weeks attention grid training had a linear effect of improvement in the attention. So, the number of sessions in two weeks could improve the attention significantly. The graphical presentation of the mean values of two weeks attention training sessions using attention grid is presented below in the table.

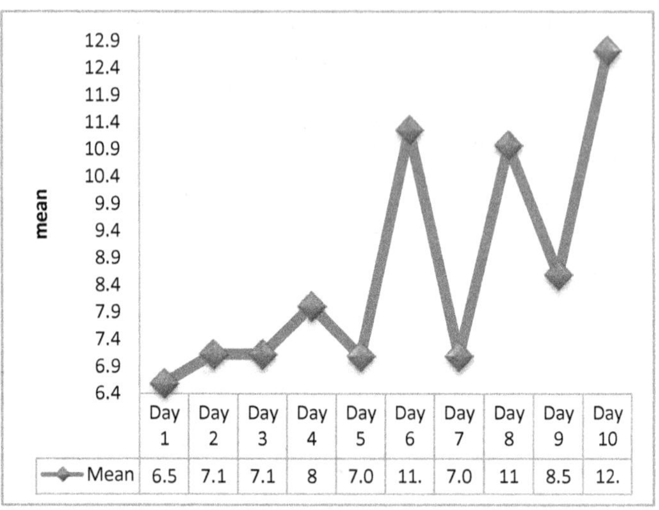

Figure 11: Graphical Representation of Mean Values of Two Weeks Attention Grid Training

The graphical representation of the mean values of two week's attention grid scores depicts a significant linear development in the Attention of the Gymnasts.

Shifting Attention Training

During the third and the fourth week, shifting attention technique was taught to the Gymnasts to improve the attention and ability to transfer the attention, which included body awareness, concentration on mind, narrowing attention and auditory attention, which indeed are essential aspect for the Gymnast's performance. The results of the evaluation of scores are presented in the tables below.

Table 47: Descriptive Statistics of Shifting Attention (Body awareness) Training Sessions of Two Weeks

Days	Mean	S D	N
Day 1	3.63	.90	19
Day 2	4.32	.82	19
Day 3	4.05	.78	19
Day 4	4.21	.71	19
Day 5	4.42	.77	19
Day 6	4.63	.60	19
Day 7	4.53	.84	19
Day 8	4.26	.93	19
Day 9	4.58	.69	19
Day 10	4.74	.56	19

The descriptive statistics table reveals the mean and the standard deviation of shifting Attention sessions over the two weeks training of body awareness, i.e first session represents the least value with the improvement in the attention on body awareness scores by the last week of the training. Numerical representation of the data, day 1 (M, 3.63 ± .90), day 2 (M, 4.32 ± .82), day 3 (M, 4.05 ± .78), day 4 (M, 4.21 ± .71), day 5 (M, 4.42 ± .77), day 6 (M, 4.63 ± .60) day 7 (M= 4.53 ± .84), day 8 (M, 4.26 ± .93), day 9 (M, 4.58 ± .69) and day 10 (M, 4.74 ± .56).

Test of sphericity was computed to test the significant difference among the Shifting attention using body awareness scores of each session, and the results are presented in the table below.

Table 48: Mauchly's Test

Within Subjects Effect	Mauchly's W	X^2	Df	Sig.	Epsilon		
					Greenhouse-Geisser	Huynh-Feldt	Lower-bound
Attention (Body awareness)	.01	79.32	44	.00*	.43	.55	.11

* $p< 0.01$.

Table reveals that the Mauchly's test indicated that assumption of sphericity have been violated, X^2 (44) = 79.32, p< .01. Ɛ < .75, Therefore, we have used Epsilon Greenhouse-Geisser to adjust f score and the conservative Epsilon should be used to adjust the df as recommended by Girden, E. R. (1992).

Repeated Measure ANOVA test was computed to check the difference at 0.05 between the two week's sessions of attention.

Table 49: Repeated Measure ANOVA for Comparison of Means during Two Weeks of Shifting Attention (Body awareness) Training

Source		SS	Df	MS	F	P
Body awareness (Two Weeks)	Greenhouse-Geisser	18.02	3.83	4.71	5.88	.00*
	Error	55.18	68.86	.80		

*$p<0.01$.

The above table shows the repeated measure ANOVA calculations, showing that there is significant improvement in the scores of Attention body awareness during the two weeks training as obtained F = 5.88 at p < 0.01. It means that ability of attention on body awareness in players has developed significantly. So, there is influence of attention Training. Thus, the null hypothesis that there is no significant influence of attention training, is not accepted. The pairwise comparisons for the main effect of training corrected, using a bonferroni adjustment was further computed.

Table 50: Pairwise Comparisons Among Two Weeks Sessions of Body Awareness Attention Training

(I) Group	(J) Group	M D (I-J)	Std. Error	Sig.	95% Confidence Interval For Difference	
					Lower Bound	Upper Bound
Day 1	Day 2	-.68*	.17	.04*	-1.35	-.02
	Day 3	-.42	.21	1.00	-1.22	.38
	Day 4	-.58	.25	1.00	-1.53	.37
	Day 5	-.79	.26	.32	-1.79	.22
	Day 6	-1.00*	.24	.03*	-1.94	-.06
	Day 7	-.89	.26	.15	-1.92	.13
	Day 8	-.63	.29	1.00	-1.79	.52
	Day 9	-.95	.26	.08	-1.95	.06
	Day 10	-1.11*	.24	.01**	-2.04	-.17
Day 2	Day 3	.26	.150	1.00	-.32	.84
	Day 4	.11	.17	1.00	-.55	.76
	Day 5	-.11	.19	1.00	-.82	.61
	Day 6	-.32	.20	1.00	-1.10	.47
	Day 7	-.21	.24	1.00	-1.13	.71
	Day 8	.05	.29	1.00	-1.08	1.18
	Day 9	-.26	.21	1.00	-1.09	.57
	Day 10	-.42	.19	1.00	-1.17	.32
Day 3	Day 4	-.16	.14	1.00	-.69	.38
	Day 5	-.37	.17	1.00	-1.04	.31
	Day 6	-.58	.16	.08	-1.19	.04
	Day 7	-.47	.16	.37	-1.09	.15
	Day 8	-.21	.21	1.00	-1.03	.61
	Day 9	-.53	.18	.37	-1.21	.16
	Day 10	-.68*	.13	.00**	-1.20	-.17
Day 4	Day 5	-.21	.12	1.00	-.69	.26
	Day 6	-.42	.14	.33	-.96	.12
	Day 7	-.32	.17	1.00	-.98	.35
	Day 8	-.05	.22	1.00	-.91	.81
	Day 9	-.37	.16	1.00	-.98	.24
	Day 10	-.53*	.12	.01	-.98	-.07
Day 5	Day 6	-.21	.15	1.00	-.77	.35
	Day 7	-.11	.17	1.00	-.76	.55
	Day 8	.16	.22	1.00	-.69	1.01
	Day 9	-.16	.14	1.00	-.69	.38
	Day 10	-.32	.13	1.00	-.83	.20

Table 50 continue: Pairwise Comparisons Among Two Weeks Sessions of Body Awareness Attention Training

(I) Group	(J) Group	M D (I-J)	Std. Error	Sig.	95% Confidence Interval For Difference	
					Lower Bound	Upper Bound
Day 6	Day 7	.11	.15	1.00	-.48	.69
	Day 8	.37	.17	1.00	-.31	1.05
	Day 9	.05	.16	1.00	-.57	.68
	Day 10	-.10	.11	1.00	-.51	.30
Day 7	Day 8	.26	.10	.93	-.14	.66
	Day 9	-.05	.18	1.00	-.75	.64
	Day 10	-.21	.12	1.00	-.69	.27
Day 8	Day 9	-.32	.22	1.00	-1.16	.53
	Day 10	-.47	.18	.69	-1.16	.21
Day 9	Day 10	-.16	.12	1.00	-.60	.29

** p< 0.01, *p<0.05.

The table indicates that the main effect reflects a significant difference p< .05 of day 1 with day 2 and day 6. Difference of day 1 and day 3 with day 10.

Further, the repeated measure within subjects was analyzed to check the linear trend by computing the data. The finding is presented in the table below.

Table 51: Repeated Measure within Subject Analysis for Two Weeks Sessions of Body Awareness Attention Training

Source of Variance		SS	Df	MSS	F	P
Body awareness Sessions	Linear	11.29	1	11.29	11.76	.00**
	Quadratic	1.08	1	1.08	2.27	.15*
	Cubic	1.18	1	1.18	2.75	.12*
Error (two week sessions)	Linear	17.27	18	.96		
	Quadratic	8.54	18	.48		
	Cubic	7.70	18	.43		

** p< 0.01, *p>0.05.

There is significant main linear effect of training f (1, 18) = 11.76 p< 0.01. It can be concluded that two week's attention training had a linear effect of improvement in the body awareness. So, the number of sessions in two weeks could improve the attention of body awareness significantly.

The graphical representation of the mean values of two week's body awareness attention training sessions is presented below in the figure.

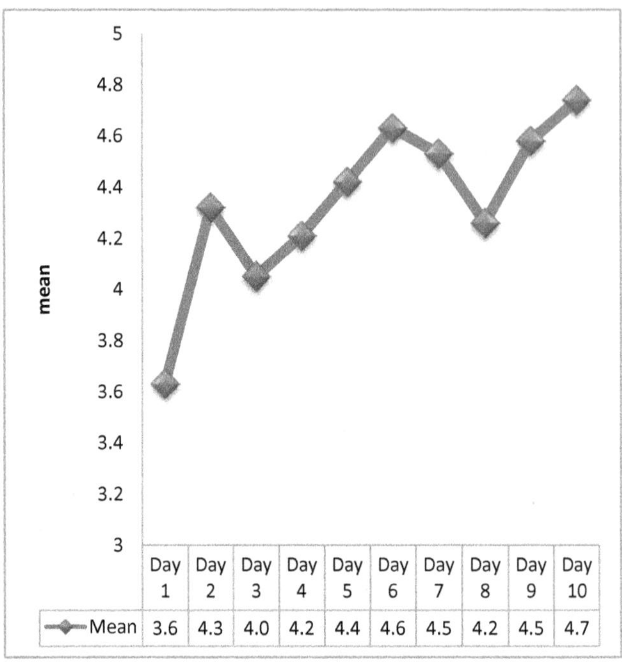

Figure 12: Graphical Representation of Mean Values of two Weeks Body Awareness Attention Training

The graphical representation of the mean values of two week's body awareness, attention scores depicts a significant linear development in the Attention of the players.

Table 52: Descriptive Statistics of Shifting Attention (Concentration on Mind) Training Sessions for Two Weeks

Days	Mean	S D	N
Day 1	3.74	.99	19
Day 2	3.69	.88	19
Day 3	4.00	.67	19
Day 4	3.89	.74	19
Day 5	4.32	.67	19
Day 6	4.47	.77	19
Day 7	4.21	.79	19
Day 8	4.58	.61	19
Day 9	4.31	.75	19
Day 10	4.47	.77	19

The descriptive statistics table reveals the mean and the standard deviation of shifting Attention sessions over the two weeks training of body awareness, i.e first session to the last training sessions.

Numerical representation of the data, day 1 (M, 3.74 ± .99), day 2 (M, 3.69 ± .88), day 3 (M, 4.00 ± .67), day 4 (M, 3.89 ± .74), day 5 (M, 4.32 ± .67), day 6 (M, 4.47 ± .77) day 7 (M= 4.21 ± .79), day 8 (M, 4.58 ± .61), day 9 (M, 4.31 ± .75) and day 10 (M, 4.47 ± .77).

To test if there is a significant difference among the day's scores, repeated measure was computed and the results are presented in the table below.

Table 53: Mauchly's Test

Within Subjects Effect	Mauchly's W	X^2	df	Sig.	Epsilon		
					Greenhouse-Geisser	Huynh-Feldt	Lower-bound
Attention (concentration)	.02	58.82	44	.08*	.47	.63	.11

*p<0.05.

Table reveals that "the main effect of training does not significantly violate the sphericity assumption because the significant value is greater than 0.05, W= .02, X^2 = 58.82, p> .05."ɛ< .75.

Therefore, we have used Epsilon Greenhouse-Geisser to adjust f score and the conservative Epsilon should be used to adjust the df as recommended by Girden, E. R. (1992). And the f was computed by considering the Epsilon of Greenhouse-Geisser adjusted.

Table 54: Repeated Measure ANOVA for Comparison of Means During Two Weeks of Shifting Attention (Concentration) Training

Source		SS	Df	MS	F	P
Concentration	Greenhouse-Geisser	17.56	9	1.95	6.34	.00*
(Two Weeks)	Error	49.84	75.99	.66		

*p<0.01.

The above table shows the repeated measure ANOVA calculations, showing that there is significant improvement in the scores of Attention concentration during the two weeks training as obtained F = 6.34 at p<0.01. It means that ability of attention on concentration in players has developed significantly. So, there is influence of attention Training. Thus, the null hypothesis that there is no significant influence of attention training, is not accepted.

The pairwise comparisons for the main effect of training corrected, using a bonferroni adjustment was further computed.

Table 55: Pairwise Comparisons Among Two Weeks Sessions of Concentration on Mind Attention Training

(I) Group	(J) Group	M D (I-J)	Std. Error	Sig.	95% Confidence Interval For Difference	
					Lower Bound	Upper Bound
Day 1	Day 2	.05	.16	1.00	-.57	.68
	Day 3	-.26	.18	1.00	-.98	.45
	Day 4	-.16	.19	1.00	-.89	.58
	Day 5	-.58	.25	1.00	-1.53	.37
	Day 6	-.74	.24	.29	-1.67	.19
	Day 7	-.47	.25	1.00	-1.43	.48
	Day 8	-.84	.24	.13	-1.79	.11
	Day 9	-.58	.19	.34	-1.32	.17
	Day 10	-.74	.25	.41	-1.71	.24
Day 2	Day 3	-.32	.17	1.00	-.98	.35
	Day 4	-.21	.14	1.00	-.77	.35
	Day 5	-.63	.23	.63	-1.53	.27
	Day 6	-.79	.21	.07	-1.61	.02
	Day 7	-.53	.22	1.00	-1.38	.33
	Day 8	-.89*	.20	.01**	-1.67	-.12
	Day 9	-.63	.17	.09	-1.31	.04
	Day 10	-.79*	.19	.04*	-1.55	-.03
Day 3	Day 4	.11	.15	1.00	-.48	.69
	Day 5	-.32	.22	1.00	-1.16	.52
	Day 6	-.47	.19	1.00	-1.22	.27
	Day 7	-.21	.18	1.00	-.91	.49
	Day 8	-.58	.18	.19	-1.26	.10
	Day 9	-.32	.15	1.00	-.91	.28
	Day 10	-.47	.19	1.00	-1.22	.27
Day 4	Day 5	-.42	.17	1.00	-1.10	.26
	Day 6	-.58	.19	.34	-1.32	.17
	Day 7	-.32	.19	1.00	-1.05	.41
	Day 8	-.68	.19	.08	-1.41	.04
	Day 9	-.42	.16	.73	-1.04	.19
	Day 10	-.58	.18	.19	-1.26	.10
Day 5	Day 6	-.16	.14	1.00	-.69	.38
	Day 7	.11	.19	1.00	-.61	.82
	Day 8	-.26	.17	1.00	-.91	.39
	Day 9	.00	.15	1.00	-.59	.59
	Day 10	-.16	.16	1.00	-.77	.45

Table 55 Continue: Pairwise Comparisons Among Two Weeks Sessions of Concentration on Mind Attention Training

(I) Group	(J) Group	M D (I-J)	Std. Error	Sig.	95% Confidence Interval For Difference	
					Lower Bound	Upper Bound
Day 6	Day 7	.26	.15	1.00	-.32	.84
	Day 8	-.11	.11	1.00	-.51	.30
	Day 9	.16	.11	1.00	-.29	.60
	Day 10	.00	.11	1.00	-.42	.42
Day 7	Day 8	-.37	.14	.67	-.89	.16
	Day 9	-.10	.13	1.00	-.61	.39
	Day 10	-.26	.13	1.00	-.76	.24
Day 8	Day 9	.26	.13	1.00	-.24	.76
	Day 10	.11	.11	1.00	-.30	.51
Day 9	Day 10	-.16	.14	1.00	-.69	.38

** p< 0.01, *p<0.05.

The table indicates that the main effect reflects a significant difference p< .05 of day 2 with day 8 and day 10.

Further, the repeated measure within subjects was analyzed to check the linear Cubic trend by computing the data. The finding is presented in the table below.

Table 56: Repeated Measure within Subject Analysis for Two Weeks Shifting Attention (Concentration) Training

Source of Variance		SS	Df	MSS	F	P
Body awareness Sessions	Linear	13.05	1	13.05	15.11	.00**
	Quadratic	1.12	1	1.12	3.36	.08*
	Cubic	.22	1	.22	.91	.35*
Error (two week sessions)	Linear	15.54	18	.86		
	Quadratic	5.99	18	.33		
	Cubic	4.23	18	.24		

** p< 0.01, *p<0.05.

There is significant main linear effect of training f (1, 18) = 15.11 p< 0.01. It can be concluded that two week's attention training had a linear effect of improvement in the concentration. So, the number of sessions in two weeks could improve the attention of concentration on mind significantly.

The graphical representation of the mean values of two weeks body awareness, attention training sessions is presented in the figure below.

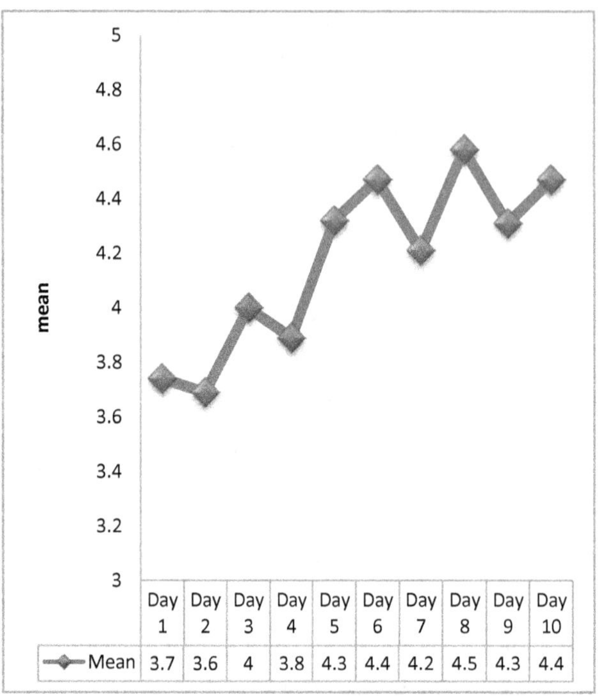

	Day 1	Day 2	Day 3	Day 4	Day 5	Day 6	Day 7	Day 8	Day 9	Day 10
Mean	3.7	3.6	4	3.8	4.3	4.4	4.2	4.5	4.3	4.4

Figure 13: Graphical Representation of Mean Values of Two Weeks (Concentration) Attention Training

The graphical representation of the mean values of two weeks body awareness, attention scores depicts a significant linear development in the Attention of the players.

Table 57: Descriptive Statistics of Shifting Attention (narrow) Training Sessions of Two Weeks

Days	Mean	S D	N
Day 1	3.74	.81	19
Day 2	3.89	.81	19
Day 3	4.21	.71	19
Day 4	4.11	.66	19
Day 5	4.21	.85	19
Day 6	4.31	.67	19
Day 7	4.26	.73	19
Day 8	4.42	.77	19
Day 9	4.42	.69	19
Day 10	4.52	.61	19

The descriptive statistics table reveals the mean and the standard deviation of shifting Attention sessions over the two weeks training for narrowing attention, i.e first session represents the least value with the improvement in the narrow attention scores by the last week of the training. Numerical representation of the data, day 1 (M, 3.74 ± .81), day 2 (M, 3.89 ± .81), day 3 (M, 4.21 ± .71), day 4 (M, 4.11 ± .66), day 5 (M, 4.21 ± .85), day 6 (M, 4.31 ± .67) day 7 (M= 4.26 ± .73), day 8 (M, 4.42 ± .77), day 9 (M, 4.42 ± .69) and day 10 (M, 4.52 ± .61).

To test if there is a significant difference among the day's scores, repeated measure was computed and the results are presented in the table below.

Table 58: Mauchly's Test

Within Subjects Effect	Mauchly's W	X^2	Df	Sig.	Epsilon		
					Greenhouse-Geisser	Huynh-Feldt	Lower-bound
Attention (Narrowing)	.00	94.89	44	.00*	.50	.69	.11

* p< 0.01.

Table reveals that the Mauchly's test indicated that assumption of sphericity have been violated, X^2 (44) = 94.89, p< .01. Therefore, df"were corrected using Greenhouse-Geisser estimates of sphericity ε = 0.50."

Table 59: Repeated Measure ANOVA for Comparison of Means During Two Weeks of Shifting Attention (Narrow Attention) Training

Source of Variance		SS	Df	MS	F	P
Narrow Attention	Greenhouse-Geisser	10.21	4.50	2.27	4.81	.00*
Greenhouse-Geisser (Two Weeks)	Error	38.19	80.98	.47		

*p<0.01.

The above table shows the repeated measure ANOVA calculations, showing that there is significant improvement in the scores of narrow Attention during the two weeks training as obtained F = 4.81 at p < 0.01. It means that ability of narrowing attention in players has developed significantly.

So, there is influence of attention Training. Thus, the null hypothesis that there is no significant influence of attention training, is not accepted.

The pairwise comparisons for the main effect of training corrected, using a bonferroni adjustment was further computed.

Table 60: Pairwise Comparisons Among Two Weeks Sessions of Body Awareness Attention Training

(I) Group	(J) Group	M D (I-J)	Std. Error	Sig.	95% Confidence Interval For Difference	
					Lower Bound	Upper Bound
Day 1	Day 2	-.16	.19	1.00	-.90	.58
	Day 3	-.47	.16	.37	-1.09	.15
	Day 4	-.37	.17	1.00	-1.05	.31
	Day 5	-.47	.21	1.00	-1.28	.33
	Day 6	-.58*	.14	.03*	-1.12	-.04
	Day 7	-.53	.23	1.00	-1.43	.38
	Day 8	-.68	.22	.25	-1.53	.16
	Day 9	-.68	.20	.15	-1.47	.10
	Day 10	-.79*	.18	.02*	-1.49	-.09
Day 2	Day 3	-.32	.17	1.00	-.98	.35
	Day 4	-.21	.15	1.00	-.77	.35
	Day 5	-.32	.22	1.00	-1.16	.53
	Day 6	-.42	.18	1.00	-1.10	.26
	Day 7	-.37	.17	1.00	-1.05	.31
	Day 8	-.53	.18	.37	-1.21	.16
	Day 9	-.53	.16	.18	-1.15	.09
	Day 10	-.63	.17	.09	-1.31	.04
Day 3	Day 4	.11	.13	1.00	-.40	.61
	Day 5	.00	.15	1.00	-.59	.59
	Day 6	-.10	.13	1.00	-.61	.39
	Day 7	-.05	.19	1.00	-.81	.70
	Day 8	-.21	.16	1.00	-.85	.42
	Day 9	-.21	.16	1.00	-.85	.42
	Day 10	-.32	.13	1.00	-.83	.20
Day 4	Day 5	-.11	.15	1.00	-.69	.48
	Day 6	-.21	.15	1.00	-.77	.35
	Day 7	-.16	.14	1.00	-.69	.38
	Day 8	-.32	.15	1.00	-.91	.28
	Day 9	-.32	.15	1.00	-.91	.28
	Day 10	-.42	.14	.33	-.96	.12
Day 5	Day 6	-.11	.13	1.00	-.61	.40
	Day 7	-.05	.12	1.00	-.52	.41
	Day 8	-.21	.12	1.00	-.69	.27
	Day 9	-.21	.16	1.00	-.85	.42
	Day 10	-.32	.13	1.00	-.83	.20

Table 60 continue: Pairwise Comparisons Among Two Weeks Sessions of Body Awareness Attention Training

(I) Group	(J) Group	M D (I-J)	Std. Error	Sig.	95% Confidence Interval For Difference	
					Lower Bound	Upper Bound
Day 6	Day 7	.05	.16	1.00	-.57	.68
	Day 8	-.11	.13	1.00	-.61	.39
	Day 9	-.11	.13	1.00	-.61	.39
	Day 10	-.21	.09	1.00	-.58	.16
Day 7	Day 8	-.16	.14	1.00	-.69	.38
	Day 9	-.16	.16	1.00	-.77	.45
	Day 10	-.26	.15	1.00	-.84	.32
Day 8	Day 9	.00	.08	1.00	-.29	.29
	Day 10	-.11	.07	1.00	-.39	.18
Day 9	Day 10	-.11	.07	1.00	-.39	.17

*p<0.05.

The table indicates that the main effect reflects a significant difference p< .05 of day 1 with day 6 and day 10.

Further, the repeated measure within subjects was analyzed to check the linear trend by computing the data. The finding is presented in the table below.

Table 61: Repeated measure within Subject Analysis for Two Weeks Sessions of Narrow Attention

Source of Variance		SS	Df	MSS	F	P
Body awareness Sessions	Linear	8.88	1	8.88	15.68	.00**
	Quadratic	.38	1	.38	1.28	.27*
	Cubic	.33	1	.33	2.46	.13*
Error (two week sessions)	Linear	10.19	18	.57		
	Quadratic	5.37	18	.29		
	Cubic	2.44	18	.14		

** p< 0.01, *p<0.05.

There is significant linear effect of training f (1, 18) = 15.68 p< 0.01. It can be concluded that two weeks attention training had a linear effect of improvement in the narrowing attention. So, the number of sessions in two weeks could improve the narrow attention significantly.

The graphical representation of the mean values of two weeks narrow attention training sessions is presented in the figure below.

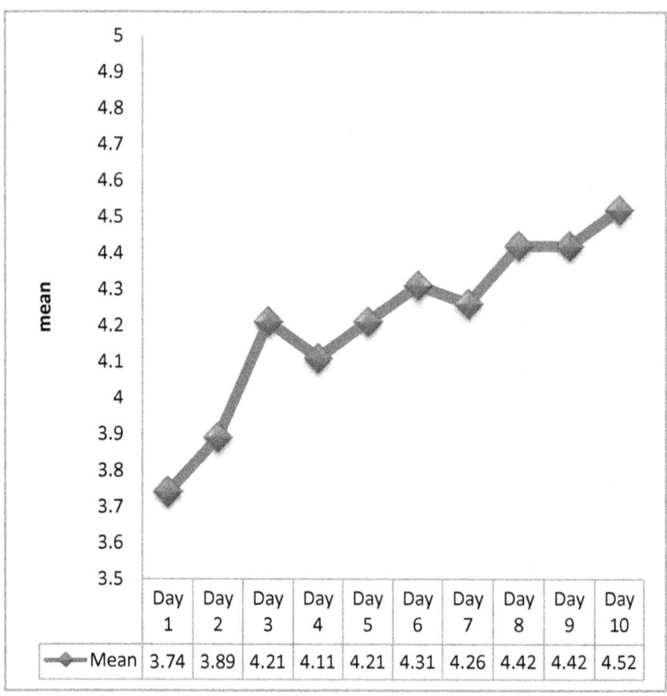

Figure 14: Graphical Representation of Mean Values of Two Weeks Narrow Attention Training

The graphical representation of the mean values of two weeks Narrow attention scores depicts a significant linear development in the Attention of the players.

Table 62: Descriptive Statistics of Shifting Attention (Auditory) Training Sessions of Two Weeks

Days	Mean	S D	N
Day 1	3.95	.91	19
Day 2	4.37	.76	19
Day 3	4.37	.76	19
Day 4	4.37	.59	19
Day 5	4.48	.61	19
Day 6	4.48	.84	19
Day 7	4.48	.70	19
Day 8	4.53	.61	19
Day 9	4.37	.68	19
Day 10	4.63	.59	19

The descriptive statistics table reveals the mean and the standard deviation of shifting Attention sessions over the two weeks training of listening skills, i.e first session represents the least value with the improvement in the attention using auditory scores by the last week of the training.

Numerical representation of the data, day 1 (M, 3.95 ± .91), day 2 (M, 4.37 ± .76), day 3 (M, 4.37 ± .76), day 4 (M, 4.37 ± .59), day 5 (M, 4.48 ± .61), day 6 (M, 4.46 ± .84) day 7 (M= 4.48 ± .70), day 8 (M, 4.53 ± .61), day 9 (M, 4.37 ± .68) and day 10 (M, 4.63 ± .59).

To test if there is a significant difference among the day's scores, repeated measure was computed and the results are presented in the table below.

Table 63: Mauchly's Test

Within Subjects Effect	Mauchly's W	X^2	Df	Sig.	Epsilon		
					Greenhouse-Geisser	Huynh-Feldt	Lower-bound
Attention (Body awareness)	.00	89.45	44	.00*	.49	.67	.11

* p< 0.01.

Table reveals that the Mauchly's test indicated that assumption of sphericity have been violated, X^2 (44) = 89.45, p< .01. Therefore, df were corrected using Greenhouse-Geisser estimates of sphericity ε <0.75.Further F test was computed by considering the Epsilon of Greenhouse-Geisser adjusted to check the difference at 0.05 between the sessions of attention using auditory's two weeks scores.

Table 64: Repeated Measure ANOVA for Comparison of Means during Two Weeks of Shifting Attention (Auditory) Training

Source		SS	Df	MS	F	P
Body awareness	Greenhouse-Geisser	5.60	4.43	1.26	3.63	.01*
Greenhouse-Geisser (Two Weeks)	Error	55.18	68.86	.80		

*p<0.01.

The above table shows the repeated measure ANOVA calculations, showing that there is significant improvement in the scores of listening Attention during the two weeks training as obtained F = 3.63 at p < 0.01. It means that ability of listening attention in players has developed significantly. So, there is influence of attention Training. Thus, the null hypothesis that there is no significant influence of attention training, is not accepted.

The pairwise comparisons for the main effect of training corrected, using a bonferroni adjustment was further computed.

Table 65: Pairwise Comparisons Among Two Weeks Sessions of Listening Attention Training

(I) Group	(J) Group	M D (I-J)	Std. Error	Sig.	95% Confidence Interval For Difference	
					Lower Bound	Upper Bound
Day 1	Day 2	-.42	.16	.73	-1.04	.19
	Day 3	-.42	.14	.33	-.96	.12
	Day 4	-.42	.16	.73	-1.04	.19
	Day 5	-.53*	.12	.01**	-.98	-.07
	Day 6	-.53	.16	.18	-1.15	.09
	Day 7	-.53*	.12	.01**	-.98	-.07
	Day 8	-.58	.16	.08	-1.19	.04
	Day 9	-.42	.16	.73	-1.04	.19
	Day 10	-.68*	.17	.04*	-1.35	-.02
Day 2	Day 3	.00	.15	1.00	-.59	.59
	Day 4	.00	.13	1.00	-.51	.51
	Day 5	-.11	.13	1.00	-.61	.40
	Day 6	-.11	.20	1.00	-.88	.67
	Day 7	-.11	.15	1.00	-.69	.48
	Day 8	-.16	.12	1.00	-.60	.29
	Day 9	.00	.19	1.00	-.73	.73
	Day 10	-.26	.13	1.00	-.76	.24
Day 3	Day 4	.00	.11	1.00	-.42	.42
	Day 5	-.11	.11	1.00	-.51	.30
	Day 6	-.11	.13	1.00	-.61	.40
	Day 7	-.11	.07	1.00	-.39	.18
	Day 8	-.16	.14	1.00	-.69	.38
	Day 9	.00	.15	1.00	-.59	.59
	Day 10	-.26	.17	1.00	-.92	.39
Day 4	Day 5	-.11	.07	1.00	-.39	.17
	Day 6	-.11	.15	1.00	-.69	.48
	Day 7	-.11	.10	1.00	-.51	.30
	Day 8	-.16	.09	1.00	-.49	.17
	Day 9	.00	.13	1.00	-.51	.51
	Day 10	-.26	.10	.93	-.66	.14
Day 5	Day 6	.00	.13	1.00	-.51	.51
	Day 7	.00	.08	1.00	-.30	.29
	Day 8	-.05	.09	1.00	-.41	.31
	Day 9	.11	.13	1.00	-.40	.61

Table 65 continue: Pairwise Comparisons Among Two Weeks Sessions of Listening Attention Training

(I) Group	(J) Group	M D (I-J)	Std. Error	Sig.	95% Confidence Interval For Difference	
					Lower Bound	Upper Bound
	Day 10	-.16	.12	1.00	-.60	.29
Day 6	Day 7	.00	.11	1.00	-.42	.42
	Day 8	-.05	.16	1.00	-.68	.57
	Day 9	.11	.13	1.00	-.39	.61
	Day 10	-.16	.17	1.00	-.84	.52
Day 7	Day 8	-.05	.12	1.00	-.52	.41
	Day 9	.11	.11	1.00	-.30	.51
	Day 10	-.16	.14	1.00	-.69	.38
Day 8	Day 9	.16	.14	1.00	-.38	.69
	Day 10	-.11	.07	1.00	-.39	.18
Day 9	Day 10	-.26	.13	1.00	-.76	.24

** $p< 0.01$, * $p<0.05$.

The table indicates that the main effect reflects a significant difference $p< .05$ of day 1 with day 5, day 7 and day 10.

Further, the repeated measure within subjects was analyzed to check the linear trend by computing the data. The finding is presented in the table below.

Table 66: Repeated Measure within Subject Analysis for Two Weeks Sessions of Auditory Attention

"Source of Variance"		SS	df	MSS	f	p
Body awareness Sessions	Linear	3.04	1	3.04	9.76	.01**
	Quadratic	.74	1	.74	3.44	.08*
	Cubic	.88	1	.88	5.49	.03*
Error (two week sessions)	Linear	5.60	18	.31		
	Quadratic	3.86	18	.22		
	Cubic	2.89	18	.16		

** $p< 0.01$, * $p<0.05$.

There is significant linear effect of training $f (1, 18) = 9.76$ $p< 0.01$. It can be concluded that two weeks attention training had a linear effect of improvement in the listening attention. So, the number of sessions in two weeks could improve the listening attention significantly.

The graphical representation of the mean values of two weeks auditory attention training sessions is presented in the figure below.

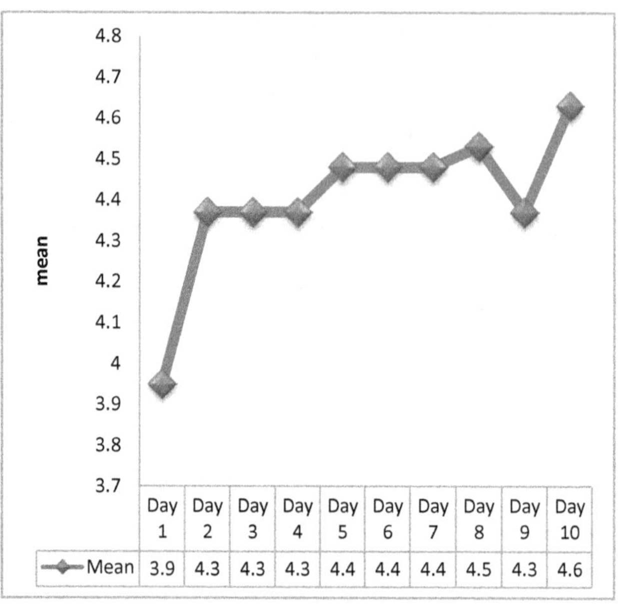

Figure 15: Graphical Representation of Mean Values of Two Weeks Listening Attention Training

The graphical representation of the mean values of two weeks, auditory attention scores depicts a significant linear development in the Attention of the players.

Relevant Cues

Gymnastics is a close skill sport by nature, in which execution is very vital aspect of performance. Therefore apart from body awareness, amplitude is also necessary to perform the movement to its fullest range.

In the present study, gymnast were instructed to use verbal and kinesthetic cues to focus their concentration on and to trigger for that cue, the research scholar instructed the gymnasts to use the cues during imagery and employ it in the real world during their gymnastics training to see the benefits.

The statistical benefits of using the cues has been noticed by the scholar during the evaluation of PST effect on the psychological skills of the gymnasts as the attention scores have shown an improvement in the gymnasts over the period of training.

The most commonly used cues or trigger points used by the gymnasts during training and competition are presented in the table below.

Table 67: The Most Common Cues used by the Gymnasts on Various Apparatuses

S.No	Relevant Cues	Number of Gymnasts out of 30 used Cue on Various Apparatus							
		Floor Ex	Vault Table	Uneven Bars	Balance Beam	High Bar	Parallel Bars	Rings	Pommel
1	Legs straight/tight	3	7	6	5	2	3	4	6
2	Arms straight	2					2		1
3	Body tight				2	5	1	1	2
4	Push/press	4	20				3	1	1
5	Late/delay	1							
6	Gain height	24	1		2				
7	Speed/fast	2	3						
8	Twist	4							
9	Rotation	3	7						
10	Toe pointed	4		4	7	4	3		5
11	Landing	3	7		3				
12	Snap/punch	3							
13	Jump	3	3		2				
14	Fast running		1						
15	swing/kick		2	4		3	5	1	1
16	Pike		3						
17	Tuck	1			1				
18	Grip movement			2					
19	Arch			1		3			
20	Perfection			2					
21	Long/body extend			2					1
22	Grace/execution				4				
23	Balance/ hold				4			2	
24	Legs together					1		1	
25	Hook							1	
26	Pull							1	
27	Weight shift								2

The table highlights the frequency of the relevant cues practiced by the Gymnasts on different apparatuses.

The table clearly shows that the most of the gymnasts at the majority of times try to focus on the legs as the loose legs or bend legs may hinder the proper movement of the body along with resulting a harm to the execution of the performance, while a very less cues are used for the execution of arms. Another important trigger used by the gymnasts on almost all the apparatuses is "toe" as clutching of the toes, makes the whole body line stretched and adds the beauty to the elements. Along with this, it can be noticed that on vault table "push" cue is dominating as it's the contact and repulsion of the hands with the vault table, which decides the future of the vault. It's a well known fact that in gymnastics "landing" plays an important role as if the landing is misbalanced or missed it may result in a zero. On floor majority of the gymnasts paid attention on gaining the height in the elements, as a good height provide enough time in the air to execute the twist and rotations and land on the feet to get an advantage of that element from the judges. On uneven bars, toe pointed, swing/kick, grip movement, arch, perfection and body extension has been focused. The relevant cues on balancing beam suits the requirement of performance on the beam as the cues used are straight legs, body tight, gaining height, toe pointed, landing, jump, grace/execution and balance/hold. On high bar boys used legs straight, body tight, toe pointed, swing, arch and legs together. And on parallel bars along with legs, arms and body straight, push, toe pointed and swing was focused. Gymnasts used legs straight, body tight, push, swing, balance, hook and pull on roman rings. The most used cues on the pommel horse were legs together as legs play an important role in the movement of circles on pommel horse, straight arms, tight body for proper support and flow of movement with press, and keeping toes pointed and long extended body and shifting of the body, as it will allow legs to move swiftly and execution of the movement will be improved

Section VII-Goal Setting and Positive Self-talk

In the present study, Goal setting statements and the Positive Self-talk statements were analyzed qualitatively as a subjective judgment was required based on no quantifiable information given by the Gymnasts.

Goal-Setting Training Evaluation

The existence of mechanism of a positive relationship between goals and performance had made the scholar to incorporate the goal setting training in the training program. Each Gymnast involved in the training program was asked to set weekly goals on the first day of every week and on the last day of each week were asked to evaluate themselves in percentage, about how much they really feel could achieve their goal on the particular apparatus or element. The analysis is presented in the table No. 69. Table is self-explanatory and represents the percentage of goal each Gymnast has achieved progressively after every week. As gymnast number one has progressed from 60% in first week to 85% in sixth week. Table further shows few gymnasts had changed their goal in the third week or fourth week probably they might have set easy goal in first week and which they achieve by the end of third week itself.

Table 68: Representation of Goal Setting of Technical Goal and its Evaluation by the Gymnasts Themselves for Six Weeks

	Technical Goals (Evaluation in percentage for six weeks)											
	Week 1	%	Week 2	%	Week 3	%	Week 4	%	Week 5	%	Week 6	%
1	Handfront On Vt	60	Handfront On Vt	70	Handfront On Vt	70	Handfront On Vt	85	Handfront On Vt	85	Handfront On Vt	85
	Backflip Salto On Bb	60	Backflip Salto On Bb	80	Backflip Salto On Bb	75	Backflip Salto On Bb	80	Backflip Salto On Bb	85		
	Back 720 On Flx	60	Back 720 On Flx	70	Back 720 On Flx	70			Back 720 On Flx	98	Back 720 On Flx	95
2	Twist 900 On Flx		Twist 900 On Flx		Twist 900 On Flx	80	Set On Hb	60	Set On Hb	70	Twist 900 On Flx	90
3	Tsukahara Stretch	60	Tsukahara Stretch		Tsukahara Stretch	70	Tsukahara Stretch	80				
					T Hold On RR	30	T Hold On RR	40	T Hold On RR	40	T Hold On RR	40
4	Yurchenko&Tsuka hara Stretch		Jager From Eagle Grip On Hb	10	Swallow On Rr	50	Double 360 Dismount On Hb	20	Jager On Hb	90	Back 540 Rollout On Flx	60
5	Double On Flx	30	Double Back On Flx	30	Double Back On Flx	35	Double On Flx	40	Double On Flx	45	Double On Flx	50
	Twist 720 On Flx	30	Aerial Front On Bb		Aerial Front On Bb	35	Twist 720 On Flx	40	Twist 720 On Flx	45	Twist 720 On Flx	50
	Front Salto Bb	30	Front Salto Bb	30	Front Salto Bb	35					Aerial On Bb	60
6	Pike Tsukahara	75	Double Back On Flx	30	Double Back On Flx	30	Double Back On Flx	40				
	Pike Gainer On Bb	85	Twist 720 On Flx	30	Twist 720 On Flx	40	Twist 720 On Flx	40				
7	Tkatchev	72	Tkatchev	75	Tkatchev	75	Tkatchev	80				
			BB- Aerial Walkover	50	BB- Aerial Walkover	50	BB- Aerial Walkover	50	BB - Aerial Walkover	65	BB - Aerial Walkover	70
8	Forward giant On Ub	10			Forward Giant On Ub	40	Forward Giant On Ub	45	Forward Giant On Ub	50	Forward Giant On Ub	50
	Front 360 On Flx	40			Front 360 On Flx	40	Front 360 On Flx	45	Front 360 On Flx	50	Front 360 On Flx	60
			Double Back On Flx	20	Double Back On Flx	40	Double Back On Flx	45	Back 540 On Flx	50	Double Back On Flx	50
9			Back salto St. On Flx	40			Handspring On Bb	20			Back Salto St. On Flx	60
	Backfip On Flx	80	Backflip On Flx	80			Backflip On Flx	90			Round Off On Vt	20

Table 68 Continue: Representation of Goal Setting of Technical Goal and its Evaluation by the Gymnasts Themselves for Six Weeks

S. No	Week 1	%	Week 2	%	Week 3	%	Week 4	%	Week 5	%	Week 6	%
10	F.Ex- 720 Back Twist	60	F.Ex- 540	60	Vt-Tsukahara	70	F.Ex- 540	95	Flx- 540	96	Flx- 540	85
			HB-Tkatchev	60	HB-Tkatchev	70			HB-Tkatchev	96	HB-Tkatchev	85
11	Round Off On Vt	60			Cut Upstart On Pb	60	Cut Upstart On Pb	70	Round Off On Vt	90	Backup Rise On Rr	80
	Dismount On Ph	60	Dismount On Ph	90								
12	T On RR	40			T On RR	50					Dismount On RR	95
			Hb-Routine	20	Hb-Routine	30						
13	540 On VT	50	Back Giant On PB	50			540 On VT	60	Back Giant On PB	80	360 On Flx	
					Back Giant On RR	50	Pike Tsukahara	60	Back Giant On RR	70	Back Giant On RR	70
14	Front One Leg	10	Front One Leg	20	Front One Leg	20	Front One Leg	30				
			Backflip Back Salto	20	Backflip Back Salto	30	Giant On Hb	10	Giant On Hb	50	Giant On Hb	90
15	Back Salto On Flx	30	Back Scissor On Ph	50	Back Up Rise On Rr	60	Back Up Rise On Rr	70	Back Up Rise On Rr	70	Back Up Rise On Rr	70
	Cast On Pb	50	Cast On Pb	50	Cast On Pb	60	Cast On Pb	70	Cast On Pb	70	Cast On Pb	70
	Back Scissor	30			Circle On Ph	60	Circle On Ph	70	Circle On Ph	70	Circle On Ph	60
	Handspring Push On Vt	30	Upstart On Hb	50	Handspring On Vt	60	Upstart On Hb	70	Upstart On Hb	70	Upstart On Hb	60
16	Tsukahara Tuck On Vt	50	Tsukahara Tuck On Vt	70	Tsukahara Tuck On Vt	90	Dismount St. 360 On Pb	53	Dismount St. 360 On Pb		Back Gaint On Rr	40
	HB-Tkatchev	60	HB-Tkatchev	70	HB-Tkatchev	70	Back Gaint On Rr	30				
17	Handspring On VT	40	Handspring Front On Flx	50	Roundoff On Vt	70	Roundoff On Vt	70	Roundoff On Vt	70	Roundoff On Vt	70
	Back Straight On Flx	20			Back Straight On Flx	40	Handfront On Flx	60	Handfront On Flx	60	Handfront On Flx	60
							Handspring Pike On Vt	80	Handspring Pike On Vt	80	Handspring Pike On Vt	90
18	Tsukahara Tuck On Vt	50	Tsukahara Tuck On Vt	60	Tsukahara Tuck On Vt	60						
	Forward Giant On Rr	10	Forward Giant On Rr	10	Forward Giant On Rr	25						

Table 68 Continue: Representation of Goal Setting of Technical Goal and its Evaluation by the Gymnasts Themselves for Six Weeks

S.No.	Technical Goals (Evaluation in percentage for six weeks)												
	Week 1	%	Week 2	%	Week 3	%	Week 4	%	Week 5	%	Week 6	%
	540 On Flr	30	540 On Flr	30	540 On Flr	25						
			Back Salto On Bb	30	Back Salto On Bb	60						
19	Pike On Vt	50	Pike On Vt	50	Pike On Vt	50			Pike On Vt	50	Pike On Vt	60
			Backflip On Bb	50	Backflip On Bb	50			Backflip On Bb	50	Backflip On Bb	60
	Front Stretch On Flx	50			Front Stretch On Flx	50	Front Stretch On Flx	60	Front Stretch On Flx	50	Front Stretch On Flx	60
20	Pike On Vt	20			Pike On Vt	30			Pike On Vt	50	Pike On Vt	50
	Backflip On Flx	10	Backflip Salto On Flx				Backflip Salto On Flx		Backflip Salto On Flx		Backflip Salto On Flx	20
21	Backflip On Flx	20	Backflip On Flx	40	Backflip On Flx	80	Handspring On Vt	20	Handspring On Vt	40		
	Front Salto On Tramp	20	Front Salto On Tramp	60	Front Salto On Tramp	100						
22	Handspring On VT	90			Cast On PB	80	Cast On PB	70	Front Up Rise On RR	30	Front Up Rise On RR	60
	Backup Rise On Hb	40										
23	Backflip Back on Flx		Scale On Toe On Bb	70	Frontwalkover On BB	60						
	Handspring On VT	80	Leap To Stag on Flx	50	Backwalkover On BB	50						

Table 68 Continue: Representation of Goal Setting of Technical Goal and its Evaluation by the Gymnasts Themselves for Six Weeks

S.No	Technical Goals (Evaluation in percentage for six weeks)											
	Week 1	%	Week 2	%	Week 3	%	Week 4	%	Week 5	%	Week 6	%
24	Forward 540 On Flx	80	Tkatchev On Hb	30			Back 360 On Flx	70				
	Back Giant On Rr	40	Back Giant On Rr	30	Back Giant On Rr	90						
	Forward Stretch	40	Forward Stretch	30								
	Tsukahara	20	Tsukahara	30								
25	Handspring On VT	70	Front Salto On Flr	80	Backflip On Flr	70	Back Flip On Flr	80	Back Flip On Flr	80	Back Flip On Flr	80
26	Front On Flx	80	Front On Flx	90	Circle On Ph	60			Circle On Ph	60	Circle On Ph	60
	Back Up Rise On PB	70	Scissor On PH	60	Inlocation to Back Uprise On RR	30	Scissor On Ph	50	Inlocation To Backuprise Ob Rr	30	Inlocation To Backuprise Ob Rr	40
	Handspring On VT	50										
27	Turn Front On Flx	30	Turn Front On Flx	40	Turn Front On Flx	60	Turn Front On Flx	60	Turn Front On Flx	60	Turn Front On Flx	70
	Front One Leg	90										
28			Turn Front	11	Turn Front		Turn Front	30	Turn Front	70	Turn Front	100
	Front One Leg To Backflip	70			Front One Leg To Backflip	90						
29	Handspring On VT	40			Roundof f On Vt	50	Roundoff On Vt	50	Roundoff On Vt	60	Roundoff On Vt	65
	Backflip Straight On Flx	50	Handspring Front On Flx	40			Handspring Front On Flx	50	Handspring Front On Flx	60	Handspring Front On Flx	70
							Handspring Pike On Vt	50	Handspring Pike On Vt	60	Handspring Pike On Vt	70

Section VIII-Positive Self-talk Training Analysis

Positive self-talk affirms that one possess the skills, abilities, positive attitudes and beliefs that are the building blocks of success, keeping this fact, the positive self-talk training was set in the training program and the Gymnasts were provided with the training by the research scholar in a systematic manner. The process of first identifying the negative thoughts and then changing them into positive thoughts was the part of training. In the present section, Gymnast's Negative thoughts were changed to the positive self-talk. The results are presented in the Tables below.

Table 69: The Most Common Negative Self-Talk Used by the Gymnasts

S.No	Negative thoughts	Number of Gymnasts repeated the negative thought					
		Week 1	Week 2	Week 3	Week 4	Week 5	Week 6
1	Fear of injury	22	17			17	11
2	Injured (pain)	7	6			6	2
3	Fear of fall	12	19			13	6
4	Doubtful attempts	11	12			6	7
5	Disturbance by friend	6	4			1	
6	Low energy	19	8	*Changing*		4	3
7	Others doing better	10	3			1	1
8	Study pressure	5		*negative self*		1	
9	Audience fear	1					3
10	Scolded by/fear coach	9	22	*talk to positive*		2	2
11	Scolded by parents						1
12	Lack of confidence	2	4	*self talk*		1	1
13	Junior /friend teaches	1					
14	Poor quality Apparatus	1	1				1
15	Fear of competition		1			2	5
16	Heavy/food makes heavy		2			1	
17	Poor feedback					1	
18	Poor execution/technique					2	2

From the table it can, easily be understood that because of the higher difficulty of movements in gymnastics and requirement of performing elements with execution makes gymnasts work harder and harder towards learning but along with that hard work the thoughts that dominates a gymnasts mind are presented in the table above. The Fear of injury and fear of fall are dominating along with the doubt in attempting the elements. The learning process some time gets difficult and coach may get violent while teaching, The fear of coach is also negative as that hinder the learning and training and here we can see the big number of thoughts are occupied with the fear of coach. Lack of confidence or inability to perform confidently on the poor quality apparatuses was also a matter of concern. Self doubt and feeling low, that might be because of lack of interest and or confidence, has been repeated by the majority of the gymnasts. There are number of other negative thoughts in the table which were noticed by the gymnasts and written down in the logbook during the training.

When after the first two weeks of negative thoughts identification, Gymnasts were taught to stop the negative thoughts and replace them into the positive ones, the Gymnasts could improve their positive self talk after the efforts were made. By looking at the table, it is observed that a reduction in the number of negative thoughts had started by the end of the training. Through this it can be concluded that the training of self talkhad a positive effect on the gymnasts thoughts process.

After the training was administered negative thoughts were changed to positive thoughts. The results are presented in the tables below.

Table 70: Representation of Six Weeks Self-talk Training (Process of Changing Negative self talk to Positive Self-talk)

Subjects S.No.	Negative Self-Talk	Change To	Positive Self-Talk				
	Notice Negative Thinking	*Notice Negative Thoughts & stopping*		*Self-talk after training*		*Self-talk after training*	
	Week 1 Number of Thoughts	Week 2 Number of Thoughts	Week 3 & Week 4	Week 5 Number of Thoughts		Week 6 Number of Thoughts	
	Negative	Negative		Negative	Positive	Negative	Positive
1	9	6		1	5	4	5
2	5	3		3	6	3	5
3	6	4			5		5
4	4	4			2		2
5	4	3		5	7	5	5
6	6	2		2	3	3	3
7	3	5			10		8
8	5	3	*Changing negative self talk to positive self talk*	3	5	3	5
9	5	5		3	5	2	4
10	5	4		1	5	3	3
11	5	5		2	5	4	5
12	5	1			5	1	5
13	5	4		4	5	4	5
14	4	4		5	5	4	4
15	5	5		5	5	4	4
16	5	4		4	5	3	5
17	4	3		1	5	1	4
18	5	4			5	5	5
19	4	5		5	5	5	5
20	5	5		5	5	4	5

Table 70 continue: Representation of Six Weeks Self-talk Training (Process of changing Negative self talk to Positive Self-talk)

Subjects S.No.	Negative Self-Talk		Change To	Positive Self-Talk			
	Notice Negative Thinking	*Notice Negative Thoughts & stopping*		*Self-talk after training*		*Self-talk after training*	
	Week 1 Number of Thoughts	Week 2 Number of Thoughts	Week 3 & Week 4	Week 5 Number of Thoughts		Week 6 Number of Thoughts	
	Negative	Negative		Negative	Positive	Negative	Positive
21	3	2	*Changing negative self talk to positive self talk*	3	2	1	1
22	4	5		4	4	2	2
23	4	5			1	1	1
24	5	5		1	1	1	
25	4	4		5	5	1	6
26	5	4		5	5	5	5
27	5	5		5	5	5	5
28	5	5		4	5	5	5
29	4	3		1	5	2	4

In the above table each gymnast's individual negative and positive thoughts were studied. It is observed that majority of the Gymnasts could reduce the number of negative thoughts. However, subject No. 14, 15, 25 and 26 Gymnasts had equal number of negative and positive thoughts in fifth week and sixth week. This indicates that training should be designed in a manner that each individual's requirement could be taken care. Table has further shown that for majority of the gymnasts, this technique is useful and can be incorporated in their training program.

Discussion of Findings

Section I - Effect of PST on Psychological skills, Section II - Effect of PST program on the Performance of various Gymnastics apparatuses& Section III - Correlation between Gymnast's Performance and their Psychological Skills.

In the present study, PST was employed to test its effects on Psychological skills of the gymnasts. The results of the present study reveals that the PST Program composite of Goal-setting, Relaxation, Imagery, Attention, Self-talk and Self-confidence has been most useful in enhancing the Psychological Skills of the Artistic Gymnasts. All the data collected assisted to understand the scenario in the quantity and shaped an overall depiction of PST influence on psychological skills. CSAI-2 by Martin and PSAS-G, validated tool constructed by the researcher were administered as criterion measures to investigate the effectiveness of intervention program and to record the psychological skills of the gymnasts having different level of performance.

The current study suggests that Gymnasts who engaged in PST program had better performance when compared to participants in a controlled condition (Gymnasts who did not participate in PST program). Gymnasts in experimental group exhibited enhanced over all psychological skills, skills of Goal-setting, Self-confidence, Attention, Arousal Regulation, Imagery and Self-awareness. Whereas a statistical insignificant effect has been noticed in the motivation with a very less improvement in the post mean as their pre mean of motivation was already high, this could be attributed to the fact that Gymnasts those who acted as subjects participated at national or international level and already have high level of motivation. Moreover, all the Gymnasts were undergoing rigorous training for many years. Continuing training for a long period itself indicate that the subjects are motivated a lot.

Two way ANOVA calculation of Cognitive and Somatic anxiety reveals an insignificant change, but by employing the effect size statistics to check the change in means, it can be analyzed that there is a reduction in somatic and cognitive anxiety but with small effect size. Effect of psychological training and its positive effect on psychological skills level is braced by the findings given by George Mamassis & George Doganis, (2004). Numeral studies demonstrate that athletes, who are strongly confident in sport, concentrate better, have healthier emotions, and demonstrate better game strategies, control of tempos, and performance than less confident athletes (Chi, 1996; Gould, 1981; Mahoney, Gabriel, & Perkin, 1987). Ample of the early research prescribed PST programs and tested their effect on performance (Martin, Moritz & Hall, 1999; Garza & Feltz, 1998). In consideration to a great emphasis has been placed on identification of numerous psychological skills and on instruction of athletes in how to learn and apply them (Orlick, 1990, Nideffer, 1992, Williams, 1993). Psychological skills are related to a number of desired qualities such as commitment to training, confidence and decreased pre competition anxiety (Williams and Krane, 1992; White, 1993). Zeng et al. (2008); Bull (1991) and Mamassis and Doganis (2004) have the similar outcomes.

With an anticipation of enhancement in sports performance and psychological skills a combination of several psychological skills was developed for the Artistic Gymnasts. Results of the present study, also supports the assumptions of the researcher with reference to the findings of (Calmels etal. 2003), Fournier, J., Calmels, C., Durand-Bush, N., &Salmela, J. (2005).

The outcomes of the current study suggest that Gymnasts who engaged in PST program (performance enhancement Techniques) when compared to participants in a controlled condition, depicts an improvement in their gymnastics performance.

The effectiveness of the program can be revealed by observing that statistical analysis has verified the improvement in all-around performance of Girls with 6.6% and on three apparatus out of four (Vault Table, floor and beam) with approx 4-8%. Whereas, performance on uneven bars shows insignificant improvement (p= 0.06) might be because of the biomechanics of the elements on the bars as it requires the most of strength as compared to other three apparatuses, but however there has been a raise of 8% in the performance of the experimental group as compared to controlled group with 2.29 effect size representing higher difference, (Durand-Bush, 1995).

Boy's performance has also improved as compared to improvement in the performance of controlled group with approx 0.50 to 5% on various apparatuses. The two way anova calculation results represents statistically insignificant improvement but this might be because of the peculiar evaluation system in gymnastics, in which the scores of performance has the tendency of improvement with 0.10, 0.20 etc, by improving the difficulty and or the execution of the elements which most of the times takes months to develop. For example a child performing flic-flac on floor and other performing Back salto on floor will get the same score as both elements carries "A" value i.e 0.10 but to learn back salto it takes time as it's an air born movement. Another example for a better understanding, may be to raise difficulty of exercises for example a gymnast performing back salto will at least take 6-7 months to learn back 360 a B value element (0.20) and another 6-7 or more months to learn back 540 a C value (0.30), we can see the scenario of 0.10 salto to 0.30, takes approx 2 years of learning if learned technically and aesthetically, based on the fact, GFI has planned their compulsory exercises for sub-juniors and juniors. The various countries have their levels for the gymnasts (elements according to the training age of the gymnasts) and levels of Australia, which is one of the best performer country at the international gymnastics were reviewed (Levels of Sydney Gymnastics Centre, Australia).

In the present study all the gymnasts, belonged to Sub-Junior and Junior age category except a few gymnasts who were suppose to participate at the senior level for the first time in the upcoming competitions. Keeping in mind the above fact and understanding that even a little improvement in the scores of the gymnasts which might not be considered statistically significant, can be of great importance for the gymnasts and their coaches. To know the exact level of improvement in the performance of the gymnasts those who attended PST intervention as compare to the gymnasts in the control group, the effect size of the change in the mean of pre and post performances of both the groups was calculated. The results revealed that the performance of the Gymnasts in PST program had a greater performance after the intervention i.e effect size of all around performance of boys is 0.75, which falls in the category of high difference, on floor exercise the performance is greater with the less difference, whereas on high bar it's a moderate difference with 0.63 effect size, Parallel bars, pommel horse, roman rings and vault table has a high difference with 0.77, .84, 1.19 and 1.28 effect size respectively. The gymnasts and their coaches had also expressed that their performance has begin to improve with PST imparted by the scholar.

Improvement in performance is supported by the findings given by Calmels, C., & Fournier, J.(1999). A number of studies and as above discussed PST effect on psychological skills show that athletes who are strongly confident in sport, concentrate better, have healthier emotions, and demonstrate better game strategies, control over temperaments, have better performance than less confident athletes (Chi, 1996; Gould, 1981; Mahoney, Gabriel, & Perkin, 1987). With the related approach of psychological skills and performance, study reviews of 20 published studies till 1989, (Loehr, 1994; Weinberg, 1988) are in positively support of influence on performance. Vealey (1994), Weinberg &Comar (1994), (Cox, 2007).

Further to test the relation between the psychological skills and gymnast's performance, correlation was tested. Findings revealed a significant relationship between total psychological skills and performance of male and females. Because six mental skills's training was given together in a form of PST program, through this it became easy to understand the most effective and least effective skills on the performance. The findings of this study are consistent to the several studies, Cainey, (2009), Drista (2009), Thorsen (2005), Sui et al. (2008), Uemura (2005), Salmon (2001), Kenneth and Matthew (2009), Durand-Bush et al. (2001), Fletcher and Hanton, (2001). In present study, out of six psychological skills only arousal regulation, Imagery and self-confidence have a statistical significant relation with all the apparatuses of the boys except floor exercise, as movements on floor are a series of air born elements, which might take more time to show the significant affect, with attention, motivation and self awareness have no significant relation with none of the apparatuses. However, total psychological package has a significant relation with overall performance and all the apparatuses except floor and vault table.

In case of girl's performance all the psychological skills except goal-setting and motivation have a significant relation with the performance of the girls on several apparatuses. Most importantly the total PST program has a significant relation with the overall performance of the female gymnasts. It can be supported, with the fact that the elite and non-elite athletes can be differentiated on the basis of their mental skills, better psychological skills are related to the better performance and a positive relationship exists between the both, (Williams & Krane,

2001, Michael Sheard& Jim Golby (2006), Bhambri, P.K. Dhillon and S.P Sahni, (2005). So it is evident from the results that the improvement in Psychological skills of the athletes, initiates the improvement in their performance (Williams &Krane, 2001), Sheard&Golby (2006),which was the main objective of the present study, the improvement in performance of the gymnasts might be the initiation of the improvement of their performances following PST training.

Section IV-Effect of Relaxation Training

In the present study, the gymnasts were introduced to Breathing easy exercises, Breathe Regulation Techniques, Mantra meditation, progressive muscle relaxation, and autogenic training. Their relaxation state was measured by monitoring Pulse rate, Respiration Rate and through a scale where gymnasts used to mark themselves according to their present state of calmness to tension on a scale of 1 to 8 to check if there is any effect of each session of relaxation training on the gymnasts. The descriptive analysis and the graphical representations reveals that there is a reduction in pulse, respiration and tense rate, after completing every days relaxation sessions, with a statistically insignificant change in the pulse, respiration except week 2, and the tension rate in except week 3 & 4, out of six weeks training, probably because of the shorter period of various techniques interventions.

Significant changes have been observed by calculating the Effect sizes for the different treatments (e.g., Breathing easy exercises, Breathe Regulation Techniques, Mantra meditation, progressive muscle relaxation, and autogenic training) were calculated. Most of the treatments produced significantly larger effect size in the reduction of pulse rate, respiratory rate and tension level, which with support of the results of effect of PST on psychological skills, measured by PSAS, Arousal level has significant higher effect size along with the results of CSAI-2 in support by revealing, that cognitive and somatic anxiety has been reduced with small mean effect size. There are several studies in support, Eppley KR, Abrams AI, Shear J. (1989), Jorge Cottyn, Dirk De Clercq, (2006),Tim Woodman & Lew Hardy, (2011), Athan, A. N. & Sampson, U. I. (2013).

It has been discussed thoroughly in chapter one, that how difficult the movement are in gymnastics and what makes the gymnasts so anxious, "When anxious, nervous or worried, an increase in the rate and depth of breathing often occurs. That is, we 'over breathe', and take in more oxygen than the body needs. This upsets the balance between oxygen and CO2. When our breathing rate increases, a number of other physical changes occur in the body to make up for the imbalance. These changes cause the unpleasant physical sensations we experience when anxious", Barlow, D.H., Raffa, S.D., Cohen, E.M. (2002). Keeping in view the same, it was a great matter of concern to introduce the gymnasts with several relaxation exercises, which, indeed can be used by them before and during training/competition by themselves to relax themselves and calm down to perform in an optimum state for better results as they have proved to be effective in reducing the tension and controlling the breathe. Gould D, Udry E. (1994), Athan, A. N. & Sampson, U. I. (2013), Daniel Gould , Robert C. Eklund & Susan A. Jackson (2013).

The training of relaxation techniques can be considered as effective and useful. The human normal respiration rate is 16 to 20 breaths per minute and pulse rate is anywhere between 70 and 80 beats per minute, through regular training, we may have a reduced normal heart rates near 50-65 beats per minute and reduced respiratory rate by 4-7 breaths per minutes through chronic effects, (Green, 2003),

(http://www.stress-management-for-peakperformance.com/breathing-exercises.html). Time to adapt the physiological changes in the body through relaxation training depends upon the amount of time spent in training, (Sara W. Lazar et al. 2005). That is the reason many of the studies of relaxation therapy have followed for weeks or months longer studies. Lahmann C, Henningsen P, Schulz C, et al., 2010. The present study also suggest the same, the resting respiratory rate recorded on day 1 was 20.37 which was reduced by 1.81 breath on an average, tension reduced by 5.5% after the completion of six weeks relaxation training. A regular acute reduction in the pulse was noticed after each relaxation session but no chronic effect has been noticed as for a chronic effects a long term cardiovascular training must be administered on regular basis, Zondi, (2013).

Section V-Effect of Imagery Training

Mental imagery as an integral part of PST was incorporated in the program, to assess the imagery training learning with vividness, auditory, kinesthetic and mood sense. The positively significant results have been noticed in all the four cases when compared the first day training scores with the last week training scores. An improvement in the vividness, Calmels, C., Holmes, P., Berthoumieux, C., & Singer, R.S (2004), auditory, kinesthetic sense (most important in gymnastics) and mood senses have been presented. In the present study, imagery has a positive relation with performance of boys and girls in almost all the apparatuses except floor and girl's floor and vault, in support of studies by (Hall &Erffemeyer, 1983; Onestak, 1997), karate (Weinberg, Seabourne, & Jackson, 1981), serving in tennis (Noel, 1980), racquetball (Gray, 1990), and golf, track and field, gymnastics, and diving (Lohr&Scogin, 1998). This could be the cause of the fact that imagery occurs when the relevant object, event, or scene is not actually present to the senses i.e "seeing in the mind's eye," "hearing in the head," "imagining the feel of," etc. Imagery is an experience similar to a sensory experience (visual, kinesthetic, auditory, tactile and olfactory). It involves moods and emotions, but arising in the absence of the usual external stimuli as sensing the movement of your body, apparatus etc., Plessinger A, (2007), as we "in turn physiologically creating neural patterns in your brain, just as if had physically performed the action. These patterns are similar to small tracks engraved in the brain cells which can ultimately enable an athlete to perform physical feats by simply mentally practicing the move and enhancement in the senses for practicing imagery in the brain directly leads to improvement in the sports performance", Eccles (1958).

The above results of the present study gets more reliable with the support of the findings PSAS, in which it is evident from the results that a significant difference was found in the Imagery with in pre and post trails i.e before and after training between experimental and control group's imagery differ significantly. On the basis of the above, it can be concluded that there is positive effect of imagery training on the performance of the gymnasts (PST intervention and physical training) on all the apparatuses with small to higher mean effect size as compare to the gymnasts in controlled group. Calmels, C., & Fournier, J. (1999) study is in support, Moritz, Hall, Martin and Vadocz (cited in Hale et al., 2005), Jackson and Csikszentmihalyi (1999), Hale et al., (2005); Kremer & Moran, (2008); Vealey & Greenleaf, (2006). "In addition to physical practice, mental practice is effective on participants in development of skill acquisition component. Several studies Leonardo (1995), Yaguez et al. (1998), Cumming and Hall (2002), Hall (2002), Hill et al. (2003), Dijkerman et al. (2004) and Sanders et al. (2004) have confirmed these findings. They have shown in separate studies that mental practice can improve motor learning. However, there are other studies in mental practice learning and acquisition of motor skills that are viewed as ineffective. Ryan and Simon (1982) showed that mental practice has no effect on motor skill learning. Mulder at al. (2004) showed mental exercise has no effect on learning of a new motor task. Although Nowicki (1995) believes that the ineffectual of mental practice in learning motor skills resulting from the wrong implementation. In other words, he and other researchers (Hall, 2002) contribute this matter to person's disability to imagery properly. Unlike the results of Rawlings at al. (1972), Gabriel at al. (1989) show that mental practice affects learning of motor skills as much as physical practice. Thus, Grouise (1992) found physical practice improves the performance of diving skill better than mental practice. Also Kohl at al. (1992) reported that real exercise leads to better acquisition of motor skills than mental practice. Moreover, Jackson (2004) found mental practice has less impact than physical one in learning of a sequence task. Mulder at al. (2004) found that mental practice has no effect on learning of a new motor task. On the contrary of Rawlings finding, Wendell (1989) examined impact of mental practice in enhancing spear throwing skill, and concluded that mental practice has the same effect of physical practice. Yaguez at al. (1998) reported that mental and physical practice both improve motor learning as the same rate."

Section VI-Effect of Attention Training

Literature exhibits that, attention aids for better performance level, Wilson, V.E., Peper, E. &Schmid, A. (2006). Keeping in view the same, attention training was also integrated in the PST program and a systematic training of attention was imparted, for initial two weeks Attention Grid training was used to improve the ability to focus and concentrate on the task in hand. Followed by shifting attention training (using concentration on what you hear, body, mind and zooming exercise) for another two weeks to enhance the ability to shift attention by altering both attention width and direction over time. And finally, relevant cues training was used to teach them to focus on a particular aspect while executing the elements to improve the performance.

The attention grid training shows the positive results by improving the attention level in two weeks, evaluated by calculating the repeated measure ANOVA, it has been revealed that there is significant improvement in the scores of Attention grid during the two weeks training as obtained F = 14.65 at p < 0.01. It means that ability of attention using attention grid in players has developed significantly in a linear way. So, there is influence of attention Training, several studies support the same results, Harris, D.V., & Harris, B. L.(1984). With an aim of enhancing, gymnast's ability to shift attention easily, four important aspects were trained i.e body awareness, concentrate on mind, auditory awareness and narrowing attention, to generate the full awareness of senses to focus fully at the point of demand. Taylor J, (2010) (http://www.usta.com/Improve-Your-Game/Sport-Science). The assessment of the results reveals that there is significant linear effect of training (p< 0.01), the number of sessions in two weeks could improve the ability of body awareness, concentrate on mind, auditory awareness and narrowing attention significantly. The same result has been supported by Fournier, J., Calmels, C., Durand-Bush, N., &Salmela, J. (2005) stating that PST program appeared to be most effective on focusing, and refocusing. On three events out of four (bars, beam, floor), the 10 gymnasts progressed 5% more than 11 other gymnasts who did not follow this PST program. The results of the present study also reveals that a statistical significant relationship exist between the female Gymnast's performance on bar, beam, floor and overall performance and attention skills, whereas no statistical significant relation has been noticed in the male performance and their attention skills.

Results of the current study suggest that attention training has a significant improvement in the attention ability of the gymnasts. Evaluation of the PSAS scores, analyzing attention results, reveals that a significant difference could be noticed in the pre and post performance of attention within the experiment group as $p< 0.01$, with no significant difference in the attention pre and post trials of the control group with p as 0.91. Fournier, J., Calmels, C., Durand-Bush, N., &Salmela, J. (2005), in several studies Gould, Weiss, and Weinberg (1981) displayed significantly higher levels of attentional focus ($p = .003$) than less successful athletes, (Golby&Sheard, 2004). This may support the fact that attention training enhanced the attention skills of the gymnasts, in current study has a positive relation with their sports performance, which is arithmetically insignificant but has enhanced performance of the subjects. Orlick and Partington (1988) also suggest the same.

CHAPTER-5

SUMMARY, CONCLUSION AND RECOMMENDATIONS

5.1. Summary

Athletes spend numbers of hours perfecting their physical performance but often neglect their training in mental skills, which is fairly an essential part of sports training.

It is recognized that Physical skills, physical fitness and mental skills are the building blocks of the complete athlete that produce outstanding sports performances, nonetheless we have been avoiding mental aspect of sports performance.

It is observed that at the top level of sport, where many athletes have almost equal physical abilities, the difference between a great performance and a good performance or between winning and losing is often related to mental instead of physical abilities. Even in Olympic Games and other big events, some athletes who are considered to win medal, fails in the competitions resultant of lack of mental preparedness as one of the important reasons for their failure.

Some studies of sport psychology have made it evident that mental skills play an important role in attaining excellence in sport, Harris, D.V. and B.L. Harris, (1984), Morris, T. and S. Koehn, (2004). Cox and Yoo (1995), indicated that "success in professional sport not only depends on the physique, physical and technical aspects of players but also on psychological skill. It is necessary to teach athletes' psychological skills which helps them to perform consistently and realize their real potential", (Cogen, Karen and Peter ,1996). Keeping in view the same, it has been understood that the actual core power exist in the sports psychology to make a well trained athlete a champion.

Therefore a right direction training for the mental abilities which prepares the athlete to get his/her mental set for their best performance at the required time, so training is one of the most important and difficult areas to apply to it. Athletes have to keep their energy up during each practice session, or they will not be able to win. This requires all kinds of mental tricks, Psychological skills training methods, in fact, involve many psychological techniques such as relaxation, visualization, the chanting of positive phrases to create a positive attitude, setting goals and motivation and even meditation to enhance focus etc.

Technically, the concept "psychological skills" contains two sub concepts which may be briefly unpacked as follows; "Psychology", can be described as "the study and the use of human bio-psycho-social-cultural-spiritual experiences and behavior". "Skill" refers to learnable and trainable abilities used by different individuals in different situations and in diverse ways on the daily basis.(Weinberg & Gould, 2007) Psychological Skill Training (PST) refers to systematic and consistent practice of mental or psychological skills for the purpose of enhancing performance, increasing enjoyment, or achieving greater sport and physical activity Self-satisfaction, Concentration, Arousal Regulation, Confidence enhancement, Goal Setting and Imagery.

As several positive results have been observed from the studies conducted by different researchers, using different packages of PST (comprising different variables and techniques e.g Attention, Concentration, Arousal Regulation, Relaxation, Confidence Enhancement, Goal Setting, Self-Talk, and Imagery), on the different subjects, for altogether a different period. The research scholar had planned to use the best suitable package of various mental skills, after gleaning the literature, a composition of six psychological skills namely; Relaxation, Goal-setting, Positive self-talk, Attention, Imagery and Self-confidence were selected for the Gymnasts which was balanced and drafted for a period of six weeks training program.

Effective learning of psychological skills is central to solving and preventing mental health problems, and reaching at the higher level of sports performance. PST if rendered in a systematic manner can yield elevated performances along with achieving greater self-satisfaction. PST is very commonly utilized by overseas sports person in a variety of sports settings as well as at different level of preparations of competition where as in our country the system has not being evolved to incorporate PST at top most level of preparation.

Since PST is extremely beneficial in increasing the psychic capacities of the sports person it becomes apparent then to give PST a status of paramount importance. PST is the mental abilities which have to be trained in order to attain success at any level of competition. Looking into the importance and benefits that can be derived as a result of PST it then becomes important to develop and implement the PST Program for different sports and therefore, the research scholar after having gleaned the literature and series of discussion with the advisor and advisory committee members decided to analyze the effect of PST on gymnasts.

The purpose of the study was:

1) To assess the effect of PST Program on the psychological skills of the Gymnasts.
2) To know the strength of psychological skills among the Gymnasts.
3) To assess the effect of PST Program on the performance of the Gymnasts.
4) To test the relationship between Psychological Skills and Gymnast's performance
5) To assess the effect of relaxation training on the pulse rate, respiratory rate and tension level of the gymnasts.

6) To test the linear trend in the number of training sessions has affect on the pulse rate, respiration rate and tension level of the gymnasts.

7) To test the linear trend in the number of training sessions has affect on visual, auditory, kinesthetic and mood imagery.

8) To know the effect of PST on self-confidence.

9) To know the effect of psychological Training on attention.

10) Does the self talk training modify thought process from negative thought process to positive thought process?

11) To assess the effect of PST on Goal setting.

For the purpose of the present experimental study the purposive sampling method is used since only those gymnasts were selected for the purpose of experiment who have had participated at least at district/state championships and higher levels. By using this method the scholar has selected two groups of 30 gymnasts each from the gymnasts trainees at the Bhoir Gymkhana, Mumbai, for the purpose of the study who represented the Indian gymnasts population in true manner and served as experimental group and controlled group. The age range of the participants spanned 9 to 17 years and the average age of the subjects was approximately 13± years, while years of training ranged between 4–11 years with the average training age of 6±. All gymnasts participated at least at the district/State/national competitive sub-junior, junior and senior gymnastics championships. While, five elite gymnasts represented India at international level.

Thus, the experimental Group and control group initially consisted of 30 gymnasts. Voluntarily Gymnasts attended training regularly at their respective Gymnastics center, situated in India. But in experiment group one gymnasts had discontinued due to an injury she had during the training of gymnastics and six gymnasts did not turn up for the second trials, from the control group. Finally, total number of 29 gymnasts completed the training in experimental group and 24 gymnasts completed pre and post trials in control group.

On the basis of available literature and various researches it is said that psychological skills play an important role in enhancing the performance of the Gymnast (Bennett and Pravitz, 1982). In the present study Psychological Skill are the independent variables whereas, the performance is the dependent variable. In order, to assess the significant contribution of PST towards the Gymnast's performance, in the present study the following psychological skills-Relaxation, Imagery, Attention, self-Confidence, Self-talk and Goal Setting were used. Program includes the considerations, such as Educational Session, Skill development, Application and Evaluation. Performance, skill acquisition and Psychological well-being are important variables of the study as on these parameters the scores of the gymnast's before PST and after PST have been evaluated to assess the effect of PST program on the gymnast's performance.

At the initial and the final phase all the gymnasts completed questionnaires. Somatic & cognitive anxiety and self-confidence was evaluated by CASI-2 by Martin.

Psychological skills assessment scale was developed by Sharma and Sharma (2012) was used to test psychological skills among gymnasts. The detailed procedure for the development of the scale and exploratory analysis has been separately presented in chapter IV.

Psychological Skills Assessment Scale (PSAS), test the goal-setting, imagery, self-confidence, attention, motivation, psychic energy management and self-awareness of the gymnasts.

For the purpose of the training, a psychological skills worksheet prepared by the research scholar was used, for the purpose of recording, assessing analyzing daily relaxation, goal-setting, self talk, imagery, attention and self-confidence. Federation of International Gymnastics code of points WAG and MAG, 2009-2012, was used to assess the pre and post Gymnastics performance of the subjects.

An experimental Psychological Skills Training Program for six weeks (five days in a week), was developed for developing selected psychological skills such as Imagery, Relaxation, Confidence, Goal setting, Self-talk and Concentration for the Gymnasts. Before developing the training program the relevant literature was studied and different methods for developing the selected mental skills were studied. On the basis of their advantages over the other methods, were incorporated in the training. Scholar also considered the best suitable mental exercises for a gymnast while preparing the training schedule and placed in the training program. Since, training program was developed for each selected psychological skills each variable had its own training program including various exercises to have an impact on the gymnast's performance. Since, the training was carried for six weeks and the level of performance of the subjects were ranging from the state to the international level. Scholar has incorporated more than one technique so to break the monotonous factor as well as to ensure that the subjects would show interest in learning new things to enhance their psychological skills.

The research scholar after making an approach to the various training Centre, choose to conduct her research program at Bhoir's Gymkhana in Dombivali, Mumbai as the owner of the Centre agreed to cooperate for training and had a sufficient number of gymnasts with participation at various levels from district to international level. The research scholar stayed at Dombivali for six weeks to apply the six weeks PST program on gymnasts, developed by the scholar. The developed training program was implemented in four stages namely, Stage I–

Rapport Development, Stage II–Pre PST evaluation, Stage III–Psychological Skills Training and Stage IV–Application and Evaluation.

Research scholar administered the training program for six weeks, five days a week. Total thirty training sessions were given to subjects. To monitor the effectiveness of each session, scholar with consultation to the supervisor, designed a logbook of 20 pages for the purpose of the study, the front pages of the logbook included the demographic details of the gymnasts and other relevant information regarding the scholar and the research study. Followed by the consent letter, thoroughly read, understood and duly signed by all the gymnasts those who agreed to participate in the study voluntarily. The worksheets of various variables were designed separately for each exercise to make it convenient for the gymnasts to respond and the research scholar could analyze them easily.

By designing logbook it was possible to collect the raw data of each subject separately for thirty days that is five days PST sessions in a week for six weeks PST program.

Though the psychological skills incorporated in the PST program were interrelated to each other, but a systematic sequence of order for the delivery of PST program was followed. Initially relaxation training was administered to make all the gymnasts feel fresh and stress free and function efficiently in setting the goals and further identify the negative thoughts and change them into positive ones, after positive self-talk and relaxed state of mind and body imagery training was planned followed by the attention training and at the end of the sessions self-confidence training was integrated in the PST, to provide gymnasts with a positive outlook at the end of the day, which may in turn benefit the gymnasts next day to enter the training center with more confidence and perform better.

In the present study data was collected as per the schedule in three phases from the regular trainee Gymnasts, selected as the subjects for the purpose of the study, from Bhoir's Gymkhana, Dombivali, Mumbai, India. Scores of pre-test and post-test were collected to evaluate the effect of Psychological Skills Training program on the performance. For the six variables, during PST program, every day the raw data was collected from every gymnast.

Relaxation: the data was collected every day before and after relaxation training, in the form of pulse, respiratory rate and tension level of the gymnasts. The gymnasts counted their own pulse and respiration rate on the command of scholar and marked themselves on the tension scale based on the present condition.

Goal-setting: the gymnasts used to set their technical and physical goals every Monday with a target date, after setting the goals, the gymnasts used to evaluate themselves on Friday to assess the percentage of success they have achieved throughout the week.

Self-talk: the gymnasts wrote their negative thoughts in the first two weeks of training. During the last four weeks gymnasts noticed their negative thoughts if any, and replaced them into positive thoughts. They also wrote the positive thoughts, which they had during the process of training.

Imagery: the gymnasts marked themselves on an imagery scale of five i.e no image present to Extremely Clear and Vivid Image for four statements measuring vividness, auditory, kinesthetic and mood of the gymnasts.

Attention: the data was collected from the scores of attention grid, mindfulness and shifting attention. The relevant cues were noticed by the gymnasts and used during the training.

Self-confidence: the gymnasts noted their doubtful and confident situation.

Performance of Gymnastics and Psychological skills was evaluated twice:

Pretest Performance: Before starting the PST Program, the selected subjects were judged on the basis of FIG, code of points, 2009 by three qualified judges, and the research scholar herself also is as one of the judges as scholar is an international qualified judge. Although, the evaluation in the gymnastics is subjective in nature but by using the FIG code of points, which has been formulated and developed in such a manner that the objectivity in judging was ensured to its optimum level. CASI-2 by Martens, et al. (1990) was used to measure a somatic & cognitive anxiety and self-confidence mental skills of the gymnasts. Along with Psychological Skills Assessment Scale (PSAS) involves 29 items measuring seven mental skill, which are goal-setting, imagery, self-confidence, attention, motivation, psychic energy management and self-awareness, A 5-point Likert scale is used, ranging from strongly disagree to strongly agree was completed by the gymnasts which helped the scholar to understand the weakness and the strengths of the gymnasts.

Posttest Performance: After completion of the PST Program the gymnast's performance was evaluated by qualified judges on the basis of the FIG, code of points, 2009. The CSAI-2 and PSAS-G were completed by the gymnasts. Research scholar met gymnasts at their training complex for the pre and post Gymnastics and psychological skills performances of the gymnasts as was scheduled in the training program. The general scope of the study was explained to the gymnasts before starting the data collection. Emphasis was placed on the potential benefits deriving from the analysis of an individual's strategies, strengths, and weaknesses. The subjects were informed that their participation is voluntary and they were assured of the complete confidentiality and anonymity of their responses. All participants provided written consent and were then involved in the organized Questionnaire response sessions and gymnastics trial events at the two edges of the PST program lasted for six weeks.

Both the trials were conducted by the same individuals and the research scholar, who were trained and qualified FIG or GFI judges. The questionnaire response sessions was conducted by the research scholar herself, where all the instructions were clearly defined to the gymnasts, before starting filling the questionnaire responses. For the purpose of the present study following statistics were employed step wise:

Section I-Effect of PST on Psychological Skills

1) To analyze the effect of PST on the Psychological skills of the Gymnasts, descriptive statistics was employed with two way ANOVA.

2) Further, in significant cases, test of simple effects in syntax of SPSS was further computed to test the interaction effect of trials with groups of training.

Section II-Effect of PST Program on the Performance of Various Gymnastics Apparatuses

1) To evaluate the effect of PST on the Gymnastics performance of the gymnasts, descriptive statistics was employed with One way ANCOVA.

2) Effect size was also computed to check the actual mean difference in the pre and post performance of the Gymnasts.

Section III-Correlation between Gymnast's Performance and their Psychological Skills

The Pearson product-moment correlation was run to determine the relationship between the Gymnast's performance and their psychological skills.

Section IV-Effect of Relaxation Training

To analyze the effect of relaxation training on the pulse, respiratory rate and tension level of the gymnasts, repeated measure two way ANOVA was calculated, Further, the repeated measure within subjects was analyzed to check the trend by computing the data.

Section V-Effect of Imagery Training

To assess the effect of imagery training on the imagery ability of the gymnasts, repeated measure ANOVA was calculated, Further, the repeated measure within subjects was analyzed to check the trend by computing the data.

Section VI-Attention Training

To analyze the effect of attention training, repeated measure ANOVA was calculated, further, the repeated measure within subjects was analyzed to check the trend by computing the data.

Section VII-Self-Talk and Goal-Setting

Content analysis was employed in the assessment of self-talk and Goal-setting.

Section VIII-Questionnaire Development

For the development of PSAS questionnaire, exploratory factor analysis was employed separately on each sub scale.

5.2.   Conclusion

Within the limitation of the study the following conclusions were drawn:

Section I-Effect of PST on Psychological Skills

1) The result of the current study suggests that Gymnasts who engaged in PST program (performance enhancement Techniques) when compared to participants in a controlled condition, depicts an improvement in their performance.

Section II-Effect of PST Program on the Performance of Various Gymnastics Apparatuses

1) The all around performance of Girls with 6.6% and on three apparatus out of four (Vault Table, floor and beam) with approx 4-8%. Whereas, performance on uneven bars shows insignificant improvement (p= 0.06).

2) In comparison to the controlled group, the performance of experimental group has been raised by 8%.

3) The boy's performance has improved more as compare to improvement in the performance of controlled group with approx 0.50 to 5% on various apparatuses.

4) Gymnasts in PST program had a greater performance after the intervention. i.e. effect size of all around performance of boys is 0.75, which falls in the category of high difference.

Section III-Correlation between Gymnast's Performance and their Psychological Skills

1) Out of six psychological skills only arousal regulation, Imagery and self-confidence have a statistical significant relation with all the apparatuses of the boys except floor exercise.

2) Attention, motivation and self awareness have no significant relation with none of the apparatuses.

3) Total psychological package has a significant relation with overall performance on all the apparatuses except floor and vault table.

4) In case of girls performance all the psychological skills except goal-setting and motivation have a significant relation with the performance of the girls on several apparatuses. Most importantly, the total PST program has a significant relation with the overall performance of the female gymnasts.

Section IV-Effect of Relaxation Training

1) The descriptive analysis and the graphical representations reveals that there is a reduction in pulse, respiration and tense rate, after completing every days relaxation sessions, with a statistically insignificant change in the pulse, respiration except week 2, and the tension rate in except week 3& 4, out of six weeks training.

2) Significant changes have been observed by calculating the Effect sizes for the different treatments (e.g., Breathing easy exercises, Breathe Regulation Techniques, Mantra meditation, progressive muscle relaxation, and autogenic training).

3) A regular acute reduction in the pulse was noticed after each relaxation session but no chronic effect has been noticed.

Section V-Imagery

1) The positive significant results of improvement has been noticed in vividness, auditory, mood and kinesthetic sense when compared the first day training scores with the last week's training scores.

2) Imagery has a positive relation with performance on all the apparatuses of boys and girls, except boy's floor performance and girl's floor and vault performance.

3) PSAS, results also shows a significant improvement in pre and post Imagery trials.

4) There is positive effect of imagery training on the performance of the gymnasts (PST intervention and physical training) on all the apparatuses with small to higher mean effect size as compare to the gymnasts in controlled group.

Section VI–Effect of Attention Training

1) Significant improvement in the scores of Attention grid during the two weeks training.

2) The number of sessions in two weeks could improve gymnast's ability to shift attention by improving the ability of body awareness, concentrate on mind, auditory awareness and narrowing attention significantly.

3) A statistical significant relationship exist between the female Gymnast's performance on bar, beam, floor and overall performance and attention skills, whereas no statistical significant relation has been noticed in the male performance and their attention skills.

4) Evaluation of the PSAS scores, analyzing attention results, reveals that a significant difference could be noticed in the pre and post performance of attention within the experiment group as p< 0.01, with no significant difference in the attention pre and post trials of the control group with p as 0.91.

Section VII-Goal-Setting and Positive Self-Talk

1) Negative thoughts were identified to make gymnasts recognize the distracting thoughts.
2) Gymnasts could successfully learn the replacement of negative thoughts to positive thoughts.
3) Gymnasts could improve their positive Attitude, benefited by inculcating positive self-talk.
4) Goal Setting Training could help the Gymnasts to set their Technical and performance Goal for each week and evaluate their performance on the weekly basis.
5) Goal setting could bring the positive changes in the performance of the Gymnasts.

5.3.   Recommendations

1) PSAS-G may be used for assessing the psychological skills of the Gymnasts.
2) After assessing the strength and weaknesses of the Gymnasts, an Individualized Psychological skills training for the Gymnasts can be planned in a manner so that the athletes develop the required psychological skills.
3) PST can be used by the Coaches and by the Gymnasts themselves for the enhancement of the Gymnasts Performance.
4) Specific Psychological skill of the Gymnasts can be improved by using various methods.

REFERENCES

Books

1. Anderson M.B. (2005) Sport psychology in practice. Champaign, IL: Human Kinetics.
2. Barlow D.H., Raffa S.D. and Cohen E.M. (2002) Psychosocial treatments for panic disorders, phobias, and generalized anxiety disorder. Cited P.E. Nathan & J.M. Gorman (Eds.), A Guide to Treatments that Work (2nd ed.,). New York, pp. 301-335.
3. Bennett J.G. and Pravitz J.E. (1982) The miracle of Sports Psychology. Englewood Cliffs, NJ: Prentice Hall.
4. Burton D. and Raedeke T.D. (2008) Sport Psychology for Coaches, Human Kinetics, ISBN 0736039864, 9780736039864.
5. Caine D.J., Caine C.J. and Linder K.J. (1996) Epidemiology of Sport Injuries. Champaign, IL: Human Kinetics.
6. Cox H. Richard (2002) Sport Psychology: Concepts and Applications. (Fifth Edition). New York: McGraw-Hill Companies.
7. Eccles J. (1958) The Philosophy of Imagination. Scientific American, 199-135.
8. Fletcher D. and Hanton S.H. (2001) The relationship between psychological skills usage and competitive anxiety responses. Psychology of Sport and Exercise, 2(2), 89-101.
9. Gill D.L. (2000) Psychological dynamics of sport and exercise (2nd ed.). Champaign, IL: Human Kinetics.
10. Green C.D. and Groff P.R. (2003) Early psychological thought: Ancient accounts of mind and soul. Westport, CT: Praeger.
11. Hale B.D. and Collins D.J. (Eds.). (2002). Rugby tough. Champaign, IL: Human Kinetics Publishers, Inc.
12. Hall C.R. (2001) Imagery in sport and exercise. Cited in R.N. Singer, H.A. Hausenblas &C.M. Janelle (Eds.), Handbook of sport psychology (2nd ed). New York: John Wiley & Sons. pp. 529-549.
13. Hardy L., Jones G. and Gould D. (1996), Understanding psychological preparation for sport: Theory and practice of elite performers. England: John Wiley & Sons Ltd.
14. Harris D.V. and Harris B.L. (1984). The athlete's guide to sports psychology: Mental skills for physical people: Leisure Press.
15. Hodge K. (2007). Sport motivation: Training your mind for peak performance. Auckland, New Zealand: Reed Books.
16. Jackson S.A. and Csikszentmihalyi M. (1999). Flow in sports: The keys to optimal experiences and performances. Champaign, Illinois: Human Kinetics.
17. Jarvis M. (2002). Sports Psychology. Routledge, London.
18. Lavallec D., Kremer J., Moran A. and Williams M. (2004) Sports Psychology: Contemporary Themes. New York: Palgrave Macmillan Publishers.

19. Loehr J.E. (1994). The new toughness training for sports. New York: Dutton Books.

20. Mayer R.E. (1992). Thinking, problem solving, cognition: WH Freeman Times Books, Henry Holt and Co.

21. Morris T. and Koehn S. (2004). Self-confidence in sport and exercise. In T. Morris and J. Summers, (Eds.), Sport psychology: Theory, applications and issues (2 ed., pp. 175-209). Milton, QLD: John Wiley and Sons.

22. Neisser Ulric (1967) Cognitive psychology, New York, Appleton-Century Crofts (OCoLC) 561478025.

23. Nideffer R.N. (1992). Attentional control training. In R. N. Singer, M. Murphey, & L. K. Tennant (Eds.), Handbook of research on sport psychology. New York: Macmillan.

24. Orlick T. (1992). The psychology of personal excellence. Contemporary Thought on Performance Enhancement, 1(1): 109-122.

25. Singh A. et.al. (2007). Essential of Physical Education. New Delhi: Kalyani Publication.

26. Vealey R. and Greenleaf C. (1998).Seeing is believing: Understanding and using imagery in sport. In J.M Williams (Ed.) Applied Sport Psychology: Personal growth to peak performance (2nd ed., pp. 220-224), Mount View, CA: Mayfield.

27. Walen S.R., DiGiuseppe R. and Dryden W. (1992). A practitioner's guide to rational- emotive therapy (2nd ed.). New York, NY, US: Oxford University Press.

28. Weinberg R.S. (1988). The mental advantage: Developing your psychological skills in tennis. Champaign, IL: Leisure Press.

29. Weinberg R.S. and Gould D. (2011). Foundations of sport and exercise psychology. Champaign, IL: Human Kinetics.

30. Williams J.M. and Harris D.V. (2001). Relaxation and energizing techniques for regulation of arousal. J. M. Williams (Ed.), Applied sport psychology: Personal growth to peak performance, 4th edn (pp. 229-246). Mountain View, CA: Mayfield.

Journals

1. Athan A.N. and Sampson U.I. (2013). Coping with pre-competitive anxiety in sports competition. European Journal of Natural and Applied Sciences, 1(1), 1-9.

2. Behncke L. (2004). Mental skills training for sports: A brief review. Athletic Insight. The Online Journal of Psychology.

3. Bergenheim M., Johansson H., Granlund B. and Pedersen J. (1996). Experimental evidence for a synchronization of sensory information to conscious experience. Cited by, S. R. Hameroff & A.W.

4. Bhambri, P.K. Dhillon and S.P Sahni (2005), Effect of Psychological Interventions in Enhancing Mental Toughness Dimensions of Sports Persons, Journal of the Indian Academy of Applied Psychology, Vol. 31, No.1-2, 65-70.

5. Brown L.J., Malouff J.M. and Schutte N.S. (2005). The effectiveness of a self-efficacy intervention for helping adolescents cope with sport-competition loss. Journal of Sport Behavior, 28, 136-150.

6. Brown J.L. (2011). Cognitive-behavioral strategies. In J.K Luiselli, & D.D. Reed (Eds.), Behavioral sport psychology:Evidence-based approaches to performance enhancement (pp. 113-126). New York, NY: Springer.

7. Bull S.J. (1991). Personal and situational influences on adherence to mental skillstraining. Journal of Sport & Exercise Psychology, 13(2), 121-132.

8. Cairney J., Faulkner G., Veldhuizen S. and Wade T.J. (2009). Changes over time in physical activity and psychological distress among older adults. Can. J. Psychiatr., 54(3): 160–169.

9. Calmels C. and Fournier J. (1999). The Effects of a Mental Training Program Combined with a Physical Practice of Gymnastic on the Enhancement of Imagery. STAPS Journal France, 49, 64-68.

10. Calmels C. et al. (2003) Competitive strategies among elite female gymnasts: An exploration of the relative influence of psychological skills training and natural learning experiences. International Journal of Sport & Exercise Psychology, 1, 327-352.

11. Cox R.H. and Yoo H.S. (1995). Playing Position and Psychological Skill in American Football. J. Sport Behavior, 18(3).

12. Cumming J. and Hall craig (2002). deliberate imagery practice: the development of imagery skills in competitive athletes J. Sports Sci., 20(2): 137-145.

13. Daniel Gould, Robert C. Eklund and Susan A. Jackson (2013) Coping Strategies Used by U.S. Olympic Wrestlers, Journal Research Quarterly for Exercise & Sport, 64(1), 83-93.

14. Dijkerman H.C., Letswaart M., Johnston M. and Mac Walter R.S. (2004). Dose motor imagery training improves hand function in chronic stroke patients? A pilot study, Clin. Rehabil, 18(5): 538-549.

15. Drista M., Dupuis G., Lowensteyn I. and Da Costa D. (2009). Effects of home–based exercise on fatigue in postpartum depressed women:Who is more likely to benefit and why? BMC Public Health, 25(9).

16. Duda J.L. (1995). Level of competitive trait anxiety and sources of stress among members of the 1993 TOP Team. Technique, 16, 10-13.

17. Duda J.L. and Gano-Overway L. (1996). Anxiety in elite young gymnasts. Part II–Sources of stress. Technique, 16, 4-5.

18. Durand Bush, Natalie (1995), Validity and reliability of the Ottawa Mental Skills Assessment tool (OMSAT-3).

19. Durand-Bush N., Salmela J.H. and Green-Demers I. (2001).The Ottawa Mental Skills Assessment Tool (OMSAT-3*). Sport Psychologist, 15(1): 1-19.

20. Eppley K.R., Abrams A.I. and Shear J. (1989), Differential effects of relaxation techniques on trait anxiety: a meta-analysis. Journal of Clinical Psychology.

21. Fletcher D. and Hanton S. (2001). The relationship between mental skill usage and competitive anxiety responses. Psychol. Sport Exerc., 2: 89-101.

22. Fournier J., Calmels C., Durand-Bush N. and Salmela J. (2005), effects of season long PST program on Gymnastics performance and on Psychological skills development, ISJEP, 1: 7-25.

23. Gabriele T., Hall G.R. and Lee T.D. (1989). Cognition in motor learning: Imagery effects on contextual interference. Human Movement Sci., 8:227-245.

24. George Mamassis and George Doganis (2004), The Effects of a Mental Training Program On Juniors Pre-Competitive Anxiety, Self-Confidence, And Tennis performance, Journal of Applied Sport Psychology, 16(2), pp. 118-137.

25. Gould D., Weiss M. and Weinberg R. (1981). Psychological characteristics of successful and nonsuccessful Big Ten wrestlers. Journal of Sport Psychology, 3, 69-81.

26. Gould D. and Udry E. (1994), Psychological skills for enhancing performance: arousal regulation strategies, Medicine Science Sports Exercise.

27. Greenspan M.J. and Feltz D.L. (1989). Psychological interventions with athletes in competitive situations: A review. The Sport Psychologist.

28. Grouios G. (1992). On The Reduction of Reaction Time with Mental Practice. J. Sport Behavior, 15(2): 141-157.

29. Gucciardi D.F., Gordon S. and Dimmock J.A. (2009). Development and preliminary validation of a mentaltoughness inventory for Australian football. Psychology of Sport and Exercise, 10(1).

30. Hall E. and Erffemeyer E. (1983). The effect of visuomotor behavior rehearsal with videotaped modeling on free throw accuracy of intercollegiate female basketball players. Journal of Sport Psychology, 5, 343-346.

31. Hall J.C. (2002). Imagery practice and the development of surgical skills. Am. J. Surg., 184(5): 465-470.

32. Hanin Y.L. (1997). Emotions and athletic performance: Individual Zones of Optimal Functioning model. European Yearbook of Sport Psychology, 1, 29–72.

33. Hars M., Debois N. and Calmels C. (2009). Perceived development of psychological characteristics in male and female elite gymnasts. International Journal of Sport Psychology, 40(3):424-455.

34. Hasan Z., Enoka R.M. and Stuart D.G. (1985). The interface between biomechanics and neurophysiology in the study of movement: some recent approaches. Exercise and Sport Sciences Reviews, 13, 169-234.

35. Hatzigeorgiadis A., Zourbanos N., Galanis E. and Theodorakis Y. (2011). Self-talk and sports performance: A meta-analysis. Perspectives on Psychological Science, 6, 348-356.

36. Hayes K.C. (1982). Biomechanics of postural control. Exercise and Sport Sciences Reviews, 10,363-391

37. Hardy J., Gammage K. and Hall C.R. (2005). A descriptive study of athletes self-talk. The Sport Psychologist, 15, 306–318.

38. Howland J.M. (2006). Mental Skills Training for Coaches to Help Athletes Focus Their Attention, Manage Arousal, and Improve Performance in Sport. Journal of Education, 187(1), 49-66.

39. Jackson S.A., Thomas P.R., Marsh H.M. & ch.J. Smethurst(2001).Relationships between flow, self-concept, psychological skills and performance. Journal of applied sport psychology, 13, 129-153.

40. Karageorghis C. (2007). Competition Anxiety needn't get you down. Peak Performance, 243:4-7.

41. Kenneth J.M. and Matthew M. (2009). BMI and Risk Factors for Suicide: Why Is BMI Inversely Related to Suicide? Obesity, 173: 532-538.

42. Kerr G. and Minden H. (1988). Psychological factors related to the occurrence of athleticinjuries. Journal of Sport and Exercise Psychology, 10, 167-173.

43. Klint K.A. and Weiss M.R. (1986). Dropping in and dropping out: Participation motives of current and former youth gymnasts. Canadian Journal of Applied Sport Sciences, 11, 106-114.

44. Lahmann C., Henningsen P., Schulz C., Schuster T., Sauer N., Noll-Hussong M. and Loew T. (2010), Effects of functional relaxation and guided imagery on IgE in dust-mite allergic adult asthmatics: a randomized, controlled clinical trial. Journal of Nervous and Mental Disease. 198(2):125–130.

45. Landers D., Boutcher S. and Wang M. (1986). psychobiological study of archery performance. Research Quarterly for Exercise and Sport (RQES), 57(3): 236-244.

46. Lavallee D. and Robinson H.K. (2007). In pursuit of an identity: A qualitative exploration of retirement from women's artistic gymnastics. Psychology of Sport and Exercise, 8(1): 119-141.

47. Lizuka (2005) Anxiety and performance in young table tennis players. Sports Sci. Res. 26(3), 73-75.

48. Lohr B. and Scogin F. (1998). Effects of self-administered visuo-motor behavioural rehearsal on sport performance of collegiate athletes. Journal of Sport Behaviour, 21(2), 206-218.

49. Mahoney M.J., Gabriel T.J. and Perkins T.S. (1987). Psychological skills and exceptional athletic performance. The Sport Psychologist, 1:181-199.

50. Mamassis G. and Doganis G. (2004). The effects of a mental training program on juniors precompetitive anxiety, self-confidence, and tennis performance. Journal of Applied Sport Psychology, 16:118-137.

51. Martens R., Burton D., Vealey R.S., Bump L.A. and Smith D.E. (1990). Development and validation of the Competitive State Anxiety Inventory-2. Competitive anxiety in sport (pp. 117–190). Champaign, IL: Human Kinetics.

52. Martin K., Moritz S. and Hall C. (1999). Imagery use in sport: A literature review and applied model. The Sport Psychologist, 13:245-268.

53. Massey W.V., Meyer B.B. and Hatch S.J. (2011). The transtheoretical model: Examining readiness for psychological skills training. Journal of Performance Psychology, 2:3-22.

54. May J.R., Veach T.L., Southard S.W. and Herring I.W. (1985). N.K. Butts, T.T. Gushiken& B. Zarin (Eds.) The Elite Athlete. New York: Spectrum Publishers.

55. Maynard I.W. and Howe B.L. (1989). Attention styles in rugby players. Perceptual and motor skills, 69(1):283-289.

56. Meyers A.W., Whelan J.P. and Murphy S.M. (1996), Cognitive behavioral strategies in athletic performance enhancement. Journal Department of Psychology, Memphis State University.

57. Michael C. LeUnes and Arnold Bourge (1996), Psychological skills assessment and athletic performance in collegiate rodeo athletes, Journal of Sport Behavior.

58. Morris R.L. and Kavassanu M. (2009). The role of approach-avoidance versus task andego goals in enjoyment and cognitive anxiety in youth sport. International Journal of Sport and Exercise Psychology, 7, 185-202.

59. Noel R.C. (1980). The effect of visuo-motor behaviour rehearsal on tennis performance. Journal of Sport and Exercise Psychology.

60. Onestak D. (1997). The effect of visuo-motor behaviour rehearsal (VMBR) and videotaped modeling (VM) on the free-throw performance of intercollegiate athletes. Journal of Sport Behaviour, 20(2), 185-198.

61. Orlick T. and Partington J. (1988). Mental links to excellence. The Sport Psychologist, 2:105-130.

62. Otten M. (2009). Choking vs. clutch performance: A study of sport performance underpressure. Journal of Sport and Exercise Psychology, 31: 583-601.

63. Rattanakoses R., Omar-Fauzee M.S., Geok S.K., Abdullah M.C., Choosakul C., Nazaruddin M.N. and Nordin H. (2009). Evaluating the relationship of imagery and self-confidence in female and male athletes. European Journal of Social Sciences, 10: 129-142.

64. Ryan E.D. and Simons J. (1982). Efficacy of mental imagery in enhancing mental rehersal of motor skills, J. Sport Pasychol., 4:41-51.

65. Sanders C.W., Sadoski M., Bramson R., Wiprud R. and Van Walsum K. (2004). Comparing the effects of physical practice and mental imagery rehearsal in learning basic surgical skills by medical students. Am. J. ObstetGyen., 191(5): 1811-1814

66. Scott E.M., Lowther M. and Mutrie N. (2007). Identifying key processes of exercise behaviour change associated with movement through the stages of exercise behaviour change. Journal of health psychology, 12(2), 261-272.

67. Sheard M., Golby J. and Wersch A.V. (2009). Progress toward construct validation of the sports mental toughness questionnaire (SMTQ). European Journal of Psychological Assessment, 25(3).

68. Smith R.E., Smoll F.L. and Schutz R.W. (1988) Measurement correlates of sport-specific cognitive and somatic trait anxiety: The Sport Anxiety Scale. Anxiety Research, 2:263-280.

69. Stevenson M. (1999). The use of mental skills by male and female athletes: UMI, Ann Arbor, Mich.

70. Thalwell R.C. and Greenlees I.A. (2003). Developing competitive endurance performance using mental skills training. The Sport Psychologist, 17: 318-337.

71. Theodorakis Y., Weinberg R., Natsis P., Douma E. and Kazakas P. (2000). The effects of motivational versus instructional self-talk on improving motor performance. The Sport Psychologist, 14: 253-272.

72. Thorsen L., Skovlund E., Stromme S.B., Hornslien K., Dahl A.A. and Fossa S.D. (2005). Effectiveness of physical activity on cardiorespiratory fitness and health–related quality of life in young and middle–aged cancer patients after chemotherapy. J. Clin. Oncol., 23(10): 2378-2388.

73. Tim Woodman and Lew Hardy (2011), The Relative Impact Of Cognitive Anxiety And Self-Confidence Upon Sport Performance: A Meta-Analysis, Journal Of Sports Sciences, 21(6):443-457.

74. Jorge Cottyn and Dirk De Clercq (2006), The measurement of competitive anxiety during balance beam performance in gymnasts, Journal of Sports Sciences, 157–164.

75. Kohl R.M., Ellis S.D. and Roenker D.L. (1992), Alternating actual and imagery practice: preliminary theoretical considerations. Res. Exer Sport, 63(2): 162-170.

76. Lizuka (2005) Anxiety and performance in young table tenis players. Sports Sci. Res. 26(3), 73-75.

77. Mulder T., Zijlstra S., Zijlstra W. and Hochstenbach J. (2004) The role of motor imagery in learning a totally novel movement. Exp Brain Res, 154:211--217.

78. Nowicki D. (1995). Using mental training during residential squad training in combat sports: A polish experience, the sport psychologists, 9:164-16.

79. Rawlings E., Rawlings I., Chem S. and Yilk M. (1972). The facilitating effects of mental rehearsal in the acquisition of rotary pursuit tracking. Psychonomic Science, 71-73.

80. Uemura S. and Machida K. (2003). The relationship of life (QOL) with physical fitness, competence and stress response in elderly in Japan. Nippon Eiseigaku Zasshi, 58(3): 369-375.

81. Ungerleider S. and Golding J.M. (1996). Mental practice among Olympic athletes. Perceptual and Motor Skills, 72: 1007-1017.

82. Vealey R., (1986). Conceptualization of sportconfidence and competitive orientation: Preliminary investigation and instrument development. J. Sport Psychology I. 8: 221-246.

83. Vealey R.S. (1988), Future directions in psychological skills training. Sport Psychologist, 2(4): 318-336.

84. Vietta E. Wilson and Evelyn I. Bird (1981), Effects of relaxation and/or biofeedback training upon hip flexion in gymnasts, Biofeedback and Self-regulation, 6(1): 25-34.

85. Weinberg R.S. and Comar W. (1994). The effectiveness of psychological interventions in competitive sport. Sports medicine, 18(6): 406-418.

86. Weiss M.R., Weise D.M. and Klint K.A. (1989). Head over heals with success: The relationship between self-efficacy and performance in competitive youth gymnastics. Journal of Sport and Exercise Psychology, 11: 444-451.

87. Weiss M.R. (1991). Psychological skill development in children and adolescents. The Sport Psychologist, 5: 335-354.

88. White A. and Hardy L. (1995). Use of different imagery perspectives on the learning and performance of different motor skills. British Journal of Psychology, 86: 169–180.

89. Wilson V.E., Peper E. and Schmid A. (2006). Training strategies for concentration. In Williams, J.N. (ed). Applied Sport Psychology: Personal Growth to Peak Performance, 5th edition. Boston: McGraw Hill, 404-422.

90. Yaguez et al. (1996), A mental route to motor learning: Improving trajectorial kinematics through imagery training. Behavioural Brain Research, 90: 95–106.

91. Yerkes R.M. and Dodson J.D. (1908). The relation of strength of stimulus to rapidity of habit formation. Journal of Comparative Neurology and Psychology, 18, 459-482.

92. Zajac F.E. (1993). Muscle coordination of movement: a perspective. Journal of Biomechanics, 26 (Suppl. 1), 109-124.

93. Zeng H.Z., Leung R.W. and Wenhao L. (2008). An examination of competitive anxiety and self-confidence among college varsity athletes. Journal of Physical Education &Recreation, 14(2): 6-12.

94. Zondi (2013), The Effect of Breathing Techniques On Test Anxiety Among Students At The University Of Zululand, Department of Psychology, University of Zululand.

Thesis Articles

1. Bota J.D. (1993). Development of the Ottawa mental skills assessment tool (OMSAT). Unpublished Master's Thesis, University of Ottawa, Ottawa, Canada.

2. Krane V. and Williams J.M. (2009). Psychological characteristics of peak performance.

3. Moran A.P. (2004) Sport and exercise psychology: a critical introduction. Routledge, USA.

4. Plessinger A. The effect of mental imagery on athletic performance, Nashville, TN: Vanderbilt University, Department of Psychology, 2007.

5. Waples S.B. (2005). Psychological characteristics of elite and non-elite-level gymnasts. Dissertation Abstracts International: Section B: The Sciences and Engineering, 65(12-B):6700.

Miscellaneous

1. Sharma and Sharma (2012), Psychological Skills Assessment tool for Individual sports.

2. http://www.stress-management-for-peakperformance.com/breathing exercises.html

3. http://www.usta.com/Improve-Your-Game/SportScience/117746_Sports_ Psychology_ Mental_ Skills_for_Achieving_Optimum_Performance/ (Sports Psychology: Mental Skills for Achieving Optimum Performance)